6—
TUEIUY
L

★ WITHOUT KNOWING MR. WALKLEY ★

CONVERSATION AT THE DAYE HOUSE

from left to right: Edith Olivier, Lord David Cecil, Lady Ottoline Morell, and Rex Whistler

from a water-colour drawing by Rex Whistler

WITHOUT KNOWING
MR. WALKLEY

personal memories

by
EDITH
OLIVIER

READERS' UNION LIMITED
by arrangement with
FABER & FABER LIMITED
London 1939

EXPLANATION

This edition is not for public sale. It is distributed only to members of Readers' Union, and is made possible by co-operative reader demand and the sacrifice of ordinary profit margins by all concerned. Such conditions cannot apply under the normal hazards of production and distribution. Commentaries on WITHOUT KNOWING MR. WALKLEY will be found in the May 1939 issue of *Readers' News* (an essential part of Readers' Union) which should accompany each choice every month. Membership in Readers' Union can be made at any bookshop or bookstall

MADE 1939 IN GREAT BRITAIN
PRINTED BY LATIMER TREND & CO LTD PLYMOUTH
FRONTISPIECE PRINTED BY THE SHENVAL PRESS LTD
HERTFORD
FOR READERS' UNION LTD REGISTERED OFFICES
CHANDOS PLACE BY CHARING CROSS
LONDON ENGLAND

For

KITTY and EVELYN RAWLENCE

and other friends

who remember with me the old Wilton days

CONTENTS

Book I. Wine Ready

✶ CONTENTS ✶

Book I. Wilton Rectory

Book II. Away from Wilton

[11]

⋆ CONTENTS ⋆

BOOK I

★ WILTON RECTORY ★

PREAMBLE

★ THE HOUSE AND GARDEN ★

From a childhood at Wilton Rectory there comes a legacy which lasts through life. The broad, beneficent Georgian building of deep red brick stands only a few yards from the main street of the little town; yet, behind the house, one steps into the garden to see, beyond it, nothing but orchard land, a glimpse of water, meadows prankt with grey-green willows, and, in the distance, the downs topped by the Vesey Trees. On the right, a little path bordered by clipped and pointed yews leads to the great Romanesque church built in the 'forties of the last century by Lord Herbert of Lea and his mother, the Russian Lady Pembroke. It stands high on a broad terrace.

The house was there before the church, and old Mr. Moore of Wilton told me that his grandfather remembered its being built, about 1790, by the owner of the factory which then stood on the site of the present schools. This man possessed excellent and very restrained taste, and his buildings in West Street are extremely satisfying, perhaps because he himself was not easily satisfied. The semicircular wall and gateway which lead to the school have their own beauty, but they also show an unusual sense of proportion in relation to the street. This quality evidently belonged to their builder. When his own

[15]

house was in building, Mr. Moore's grandfather one day saw him stand in prolonged contemplation of its walls, which had then risen about two feet from the ground. They were not on the site of the present house, but stood almost flush with the street.

'No,' he said. 'I don't like it.'

The walls were taken down, and the building was recommenced in its present position. It now stands upon great cellars—high stone rooms of the same size as those on the ground floor—and when I had heard this anecdote from Mr. Moore, I began to think that there might also be vast secret crypts hidden underground where the first house was to have stood. The idea was romantic and terrifying. Our own cellars were frightening enough, but who lived in those other cellars beyond?

The thought of them increased the exaggerated size already possessed by the haunts of one's childhood. There they lay, unknown, on the other side of the cellar walls we saw. Some day perhaps a very heavy carriage would stop at the front door. The drive would collapse—to disclose a store of forgotten treasures.

But even without the other cellars, the Rectory was, like all houses, far bigger for the children than for the grown-ups. Children use parts of a house which are hardly even seen by their elders. There were at Wilton Rectory long secret passages in the roof, which were entered from the attic through bolted doors. Here we stepped, in semi-darkness, from beam to beam, over spaces where lay a hollow plaster floor; and now and again we came upon a complicated barricade of interlacing roof supports which had to be got through somehow. Icy draughts and narrow shafts of light broke in upon the dusty stuffiness of this exciting domain.

[16]

Then there were numbers of cupboards in the walls, in which we spent our afternoons when it was too wet to go out. In every house, an immense amount of space is lost to the grown-up people who never sit in cupboards. We had first of all the big nursery cupboard where Mildred and I played houses, each on her own shelf, for we were not sophisticated enough to call them flats. There was the vast cupboard in Mamma's room where one could walk about on the floor, as well as clamber on the shelves among her hats. In the attic was the Bird Cupboard, called from a painting of magpies which surrounded it. It was like a long low room, and we heaped pillows at its two ends and pretended to go to sleep in it. And then there was the tiny cupboard high up in the dark wall on the back stairs. It could only be reached by someone who was very small and very agile. I was both, and so I often got into it, and remained lost for hours. When I remember Wilton Rectory, I think of it as larger by all these cupboards than it ever could have been for my parents, who only sat in the rooms.

It was the same with the garden. The kitchen-garden wall made for us a long terrace walk upon which we ran and danced. When we made the grand tour round it, we always jumped the doorways, as it was looked upon as a disgrace to come to earth in the course of the circuit. If my father saw us on the wall, he always ordered us to come down, so we lay quite flat if we heard him come out of the garden door, and hoped that he would not look up.

Of course, like other children, we had 'houses' in the shrubberies, under stacks of faggots, up in the mulberry tree, and in the disused duck-house on the island. We walked, bent double, in the underground channel which carried the water from the pond into the river. We sat on projecting stones in the middle of the waterfall; and on summer evenings, we ran and danced on the roof, or sat astride upon its very top, while people talked and called to each other in the street below, and our parents strolled in the garden, innocently fancying that 'the little ones' were safely tucked up in bed.

Because of all this, no place for me can ever compare with Wilton Rectory for spaciousness and room in which to live.

In that part of the house which we shared with those less adventurous people, the 'grown-ups', the hall is what I best remember. This must be because (except for Christmas Day) it is always summer in one's childhood, and in the summer the garden door stood open, and people sat both inside and out of it, in the hall or on the steps. Here I used to hear those sounds which will always call up before my eyes the clear poignant picture of my earliest home. A church bell tolling for one of the many services: the waterfall far off beyond the lawn: the pit-pat of tennis balls, and voices calling the score: footsteps on the landing upstairs: the peculiar sound made by turning the handle of the front door: and the Blobs. I am now the only person left alive who heard the whisper: 'The Blobs are on,' or who could guess what it meant. Yet we said it every night for about fifteen years; and because, unless I record it, no one again will ever learn that magical phrase, I must satisfy myself by writing it down. Till I was eighteen, Mildred and I (and Harold too before he went to school) always came down for dessert after dinner. As we waited in the hall, we wheedled from the parlour-maid titbits from the dishes she carried out, and then, when dinner was over, we listened to hear her put the dessert plates on to the table. A Blob for each diner. One of us always stood as sentry to hear the sounds, and then, as the others skipped about in the garden or on the stairs, there came

the ominous hiss: 'The Blobs are on.' *This meant our
entrance into the dining-room and our curtseys. My father
remembered that his sisters had always curtseyed to their
parents, and he insisted that we should do so too. We hated it,
and it made us very shy if guests were present, because no other
girls of our age were expected to curtsey as we did; but now I
think it must have been a pretty and graceful thing to see. And
the more so, because we probably looked so embarrassed as we
did it.*

*Throughout the summer mornings, the hall was entirely
given up to 'doing the roses'. When we were children, Mildred
and I watched Mamie, my elder sister, doing this; and after she
married, we took our turn. It was almost a ritual observance.*

*My father was a famous rose-grower, and, by the time I
knew him, his garden had become his chief recreation. It was an
extension of himself; and as he was completely unlike any
other person whom I have ever seen, his attitude towards his
garden was also individual. He was primarily a florist, loving
his flowers as separate blossoms, rather than treating them
as decoration. He found that the roses liked the kitchen-garden
soil better than that in the flower garden, so most of them were
hidden there, well out of sight. If a flower lover was ardent
enough to venture past the onions and the asparagus bed, to
resist the call of the cabbages, and not to linger among the
strawberries, he would probably after all be disappointed, and
would find that most of the blooms had already been carried
into the house.*

*Between two and three hundred roses were picked every
morning, and they seemed to my sisters and me to be such
completely independent beings, that we called to each other from
room to room, that 'the roses have come in', as if they had*

[19]

walked in of their own volition. In very hot weather, they 'came in' before we were up, as my father knew that they disliked the sun, so he used to get up between five and six to pick them. Every evening, sheets of newspaper were laid upon the long polished tables in the hall, and soup-plates filled with water were placed upon these. Here the roses rested when they first came in. It took hours to arrange them; and, in the house as in the garden, my father would not allow his pets to be used merely for decoration. Each flower must be given its solitary honour, and the vases he preferred were simple specimen glasses in which a single bloom could sit in undisturbed beauty, its perfect form controlled by a vase which exactly fitted it. The loveliest specimens were chosen to be set up one by one in green wood show-cases; and then they remained in the large cool hall where my father visited them from time to time, coming out of the study to stare at them for a few moments, and then going back. At midsummer, when the roses were most plentiful, and again in the autumn, when they bloom irregularly, and are not true to type, we sometimes did succeed in grouping some of the flowers in big vases and bowls; but this was really desecration in my father's eyes. It was making a queen into a chorus girl. Roses picked by him were also very difficult to arrange freely, as when he cut them, he thought only of the good of the tree, so they often had impossibly short stalks which could only reach the water in the little round vases which we placed, with the salt-cellars, at the corners of the dinner table.

They were very characteristic of Wilton Rectory, those long summer mornings doing the flowers in the hall, when little puffs of wind came in through the open garden door, and we heard in the study the voices of my parents, he 'in a fuss' about something, and she trying to calm him.

The hall itself had the large square proportions of the later Georgian buildings. It was broad and high, the three flights of the staircase filling one end. The original character of the hall had been considerably modified by a good many pieces of large and somewhat incongruous furniture which now filled it. Chief among these was an enormous thing called 'Old Stroud'. This was a sideboard made of many pieces of medieval carved wood, which had been collected and joined together by a remarkable old cabinet maker who then lived in Wilton. The carvings were ecclesiastical in character—angels, saints, eagles, and mythical creatures; and this combination of a wine-cellar with a reredos gave to the spacious Georgian hall at Wilton Rectory, a look of Newstead in the days of Lord Byron. My father never thought of it in that way. He liked Old Stroud.

One side of the hall was occupied by two mahogany tables, where we did the roses in the summer, and there was a carved oak chest containing Altar Frontals, on which the curates put their hats on Monday mornings when they came for the 'Chapter Meeting'. There was a round table covered with an embroidered cloth where there always stood a fern or a primula in a pot, surrounded by a circle of photograph books. There was a rosewood cabinet containing my grandfather's collection of shells, and there were three fine old Chippendale chairs, left in her will to my father by an old woman in the parish.

A jumble of 'pieces', each with its own character, and each placed where it stood in order to be used. Appearance had not first been considered. Perhaps the total effect was inharmonious, and yet I can scarcely think so. The individuality of each of my parents was so strong, and their united view of life was so forceful, that I believe that they succeeded in wresting harmony out of those seemingly discordant elements. The house which they

*inhabited, the furniture which they placed in it, and the life
which they regulated within its walls, made a unity, which was
a definite creation. We grew up to breathe this atmosphere,
austere, yet richly compounded. Our lungs adapted themselves
to it, and I believe that if I could find it again, I should find
myself once more at home.*

I

* CHIEFLY ABOUT PROCESSIONS *

I used to say that if I died without knowing Mr. Walkley, I should have lived in vain. And now—I have. Or rather, Mr. Walkley died without knowing me. He was *The Times* Dramatic Critic when I was in the schoolroom, and in those days it was my passionate desire to become an actress. The idea was grotesque. My father thought a professional actress was as improper as a Restoration Play, and an actor was almost as bad. My brother Alfred, in spite of his irresistible charm, was never really forgiven for having preferred the stage to his seat at the bottom of the Infants' Class in Dr. Marks's school for Burmese Princes in Rangoon. Alfred was on his way to a post in the Burmese Civil Service, and he was put to learn the language in this humble position, when a travelling company came to the town. It was too much. He was 'off with the raggle-taggle gipsies' and he went through India with them, returning at last to go on to the London stage. My father minded this so much that my own secret desire was never even mentioned, and Mr. Walkley remained my one link with the world of my dreams. It was

[23]

through his eyes alone that I saw most of the plays of those days, for we seldom went to London, and our only 'theatre' was an occasional visit to Salisbury of Mr. Benson's Shakespearian Company. It is true that I was present at Mrs. Patrick Campbell's first appearance on the stage, but that took place at Wilton when Lord Pembroke had invited Ben Greet's Company to play *As You Like It* in the Park. It had been played there once before, when Shakespeare himself was one of the actors. It is curious that as a girl I saw so few plays, for we all loved acting. Even now I have never seen a pantomime, though I have acted in more than one; but my father never imagined that his children could enjoy what would have bored himself, and a provincial pantomime did not attract him.

It would be unfair both to him and to the theatrical profession to suggest that the stage was my father's only taboo where his children were concerned. He saw little of them when they were small, but when they grew up, he liked them always about him. Mrs. Morrison called us the Four and Twenty Blackbirds, and said that Papa liked to think that whenever he wanted to open the pie, the birds were all there, ready to begin to sing. It is true that though he always sat alone in the study, he liked us within call. He hated anyone in the house going out to parties. The coming and going worried him. He was truly conservative. As the family party had been yesterday, so he wished it to be to-day, and to-morrow, and so on *ad infinitum*.

He could not therefore approve of any proposed career for his daughters, and this objection extended to matrimony. He was not actually opposed to the institution in itself, for had he not himself twice married, and entirely happily? But in the case of his children, and more especially of his daughters, his standard was too high. He had an instinctive, sub-conscious prejudice in favour of Archbishops of Good Family as husbands for them, and by ill chance, none of these presented themselves. When my eldest sister fell fatally in love with a young naval officer of blameless character, her engagement was one of those things of which it is not fitting to speak in the family circle; and she only succeeded in marrying the young man at last, by the unfailing courage and determination which persisted through four years of opposition.

I rather shared my father's fancy for the unattainable in bridegrooms; and the consequence of the various 'inhibitions' (as they call them to-day) which he laid upon our youthful ambitions, has been for me a happy life spent, not upon the stage or in any of the other professions which presented themselves, not as a wife, mother, mother-in-law, and grandmother (the fate of most of my friends), but as a lifelong inhabitant of Wiltshire, which is in my eyes, the most beautiful of the English counties. The stage of my early ambitions must have proved but 'an unworthy scaffold', a 'cockpit', and 'a wooden O' compared with the grand spaces of the downs about Wilton; while, in lieu of the many passing acquaintances of a London life, I have my Wiltshire friends.

My father's early home was at Potterne in the north part of the county. South Wiltshire and North are divided by Salisbury Plain, but there is considerably more than that between them. Even petrol has not succeeded in completely breaking down the strong local patriotism which severs the 'chalk' of the south from the 'cheese' of the north, and when my father reached Wilton as a young curate, he was entirely a North Wilts. man. He had not then married my mother, and on his first Sunday in Wilton, when the afternoon service was over, he walked alone on to the hill at the south of the town, and found himself on the old Roman Road which runs from Salisbury to Shaftesbury. He looked over the country. Grovely Forest lay like a long shadow upon the summit of the downs which faced him across the valley. At his feet, the Nadder meandered through water-meadows of a startlingly brilliant green, its course marked by willow copses and by long rows of poplars. He looked eastward, and then the unsophisticated slimness of those delicate trees was shamed by a sudden miracle. Salisbury was out of sight, but before him rose the cathedral spire in all its exquisite artifice. The poplars shook with every fugitive breeze: their faint and fragile grey leaves would change and fall with the passing of the seasons: but the spire stood motionless, and seemingly alone, among the boundless downs, and, far above the trees, it carried eternally towards the sky the superb faith of its builders.

'This is a place in which to spend a lifetime,' said my father to himself, for in those minutes his narrower loyalty to one half of his native county had become a larger thing. He never changed his opinion, nor have I, since he once took me to that place and told me how he had first seen it. My brief coquetterie with the un-conscious Mr. Walkley fell from me as a little yellow leaf flutters down from a poplar.

Wilton in the old days was a great place for proces-sions, which seemed to spring up spontaneously, as if from some fundamental instinct for pageantry. My earliest childhood seems largely to have consisted of climbing again and again on to a box which stood in one of the nursery windows, to watch processions pass outside.

They were not all of them festive ones. There were those which went by regularly throughout the year, giving to the town an individuality regrettably lost to-day. On Sundays and Saints' days, when the church bells rang for Matins, there could be heard advancing upon the Rectory from Crow Lane, the hard treble pit-pat of small marching feet. We hopped on to our boxes to see the Free School boys going to church. There were about twenty-five of them, and they marched in perfect step, wearing the enchanting suits which had been the uniform of the school since its founding in 1706. So they were dressed in the fashion of Queen Anne's day, as if that good queen were not dead, as the moderns say she is. The boys wore smart cut-away coats of fine buff cloth, faced with hyacinth blue, and they had little buff caps with black peaks. The Free School boys added beauty and charm to the Wilton streets, not only when they marched in line, but, still more, when they lounged about at the crossroads, or played marbles on the pavement.

Probably another procession was converging upon

[27]

the church at the same time. This was composed of the Park School girls. They came from the fantastic Baroque pavilion in the park, which Lady Georgiana Herbert, a daughter of the Russian Lady Pembroke, some time in the eighteen-thirties, had converted into a school for the daughters of workmen on the estate. In winter, these girls wore cloaks made of lovely warm crimson cloth, and in summer they had little grey shoulder capes. They did not stamp their feet as the boys did, though they too walked in step, but very primly, watched from the opposite pavement, by the tender but unrelenting eye of their governess, Miss Aikman. She called them her 'little duckies', but she was both pious and particular, and she saw to it that the behaviour of her pupils was, like their sewing, above reproach.

These two schools were very small and practical forerunners of the senior schools of to-day. Attached to the Free School was an Apprentice Fund, and on each boy's fourteenth birthday, he was 'bound apprentice' to a tradesman in Wilton or Salisbury. Apprenticeship is a freer and more lasting kind of Continuation School than those we know now. Those boys of fourteen were out in the world. They had entered upon the trade of their lifetime. They earned a small weekly wage. But their master was still in a way their schoolmaster, and they were under discipline. Even now, many of the leading tradesmen in Wilton and its neighbourhood were once boys in the Wilton Free School.

It was the same with the Park School girls. They all belonged to the upper standards, and with their two teachers for twenty-five girls, they were well taught; but from the time they entered the school they began to be specialists. Needlework was their craft, and the making and marking of the Wilton House linen was their duty. When they left school, and each received her grown-up outfit packed in its own little travelling trunk, they were in demand all over the country as under-nurses and sewing-maids.

I regret the passing of these little schools. They did something which is not done to-day, and which cannot be done while the aim of educationalists is so to collect the children from small scattered country communities, that they can be handled in the same manner as are children in large towns. Individuality has given place to uniformity; and the traveller through Wilton sees no more in its streets the unusual dresses which did indeed imply something unusual in their wearers, and Sundays and Saints' days are no longer distinguished by the passing of those striking little processions.

But we had other processions, devised with the conscious purpose of making a show.

On Whit-Monday 'the Clubs' came to church, where they heard divine service, sang some tremendously loud hymns, and listened to a sermon from a clergyman imported from a neighbouring parish. Then they marched to the various public houses for their annual dinners.

As these clubs still exist, I imagine that they still eat their dinners, but these must be hole-and-corner affairs compared with the flamboyance of the past.

In those old days, the town band led the procession, generally playing 'The Cock o' the North', and behind it marched some five or six clubs, each preceded by its own banner. These were enormous pictures painted on silk and displayed between two poles, while their corners were held taut by ropes. The banner bearers wore the traditional costumes of their clubs. The pictures were highly coloured and very realistic. There were weeping widows being comforted by members of their late husbands' clubs, or sick men visited by fellow Oddfellows or Foresters who wore medieval dresses of the Waverley Novel date. I seem to remember a corpse laid out on a bed, and surrounded by disconsolate orphans. The more harrowing the picture, the more artistic it seemed to be.

When these processions reached the Rectory, the band turned in through the gates, and as the banner bearers pressed through behind it, they closed ranks for a moment, converting the pictures into confused streaming jumbles of gay colours. When they were all inside, my father came and stood on the steps and made a short speech. Non-club members remained outside, peering through the gates; and upstairs in the nursery, we stood on our boxes looking excitedly down upon the scene.

But the best processions of all seemed to us in those days to be quite unpremeditated. They sprang spontaneously from the Wilton soil, and were the town's prerogative. To celebrate a jubilee, a royal wedding, a victory or a coronation, we always had a torchlight procession. There was a mystery about it beforehand. A whisper was passed to our nurses, usually by Albert Musselwhite, the parish clerk, that *there's going to be fa-urty ta-urches'*, and then we waited for the dark. Those Wilton torches were wonderful, made at the Felt Mill from bundles of sheep's wool saturated with tar and other inflammable stuff. They hung on wires from long poles, and as they were carried along, they lurched and bobbed about, sometimes scattering fragments of burning wool among the crowd, which then broke up, and fled screaming. The wild yellow light shone erratically upon the forms and faces of the people in the procession, and they were no ordinary figures which were thus illuminated, for everyone marched in fancy dress. They threw themselves vigorously into their parts— careering like wild beasts, leaping like clowns, hobbling like lame beggars, banging tambourines like gipsies, or dancing like mad. Nearly everyone in Wilton turned out to see the procession, and to follow it as it streamed through the streets. Some people joined arms and marched in line in front of the band: others kept step on the pavement: but everybody caught the free loose rhythm, and swung along amid a continuous chorus of chattering and laughter. It was madly romantic; and although no doubt those processions had been organized by somebody, they seemed at the time to be the most unpremeditated of midnight larks.

The most important processions ended with a march to the top of Grovely Hill, and then the line of torches could be seen from the street, a moving streak of light upon the background of the dark down. At the edge of the wood was the Jubilee Oak, planted to commemorate the Jubilee of Queen Victoria: and here they used to light an enormous bonfire, round which everybody danced in their fantastic dresses, newly illuminated now by the roaring, soaring flames, which lost themselves at last in hanging clouds of bronze-coloured smoke.

And when all was over, and the children had been sent to bed, it was exciting to lie there listening to the people coming home—many voices in the night, and much laughter: distant shouts which grew more and more distant; footsteps passing in the street, in hundreds at first; then, quietly and slowly in twos; and at last, rather unsteadily, in ones. Doors banged. The lamplighter hurried by with his long pole, putting out the gas lamps. Window after window darkened. Silence fell.

Sometimes our processions celebrated a victory at an election, for before the days of universal suffrage, Wilton was passionately political. Except for those who have to count them, votes seem to count less now that everybody has one. When I first remember elections, the suffrage was comparatively small, yet no one appeared to be shut out of politics. The factory girls were not Suffragettes, for that race did not yet exist, but Mrs. Pankhurst herself was not a more fervent politician. The girls wore blue rosettes, and they crowded to political meetings. They ran about the streets, as we all did, cheering and booing the carriages decorated with the rival colours. Women wore dresses made entirely of royal blue or of scarlet; and Jack Gerrish, the leading Wilton drunkard, painted himself blue all over. New words were set to the popular songs of the day, and new catch-words were coined in every street, to be called from every corner. No one said, as voters sometimes say now, that they 'take no interest in politics'. Everybody clamoured to be in the thick of it—and was.

At the first election which I can remember, our two candidates were Mr. Sidney Herbert (afterwards Lord Pembroke) and Sir Thomas Grove. Till then, Wilton had been a Parliamentary Borough, returning its own member, who at that time was Mr. Herbert, but the new Franchise Act made it part of the southern division of the county. Of course this was galling to the *amour-propre* of the burgesses, who found themselves outnumbered by the newly enfranchized villagers. Moreover, the Liberal candidate was himself one of these despised outlanders, for Tommy Grove, as we derisively called him, came from Ferne, a country house at least sixteen miles away, and almost in Dorset.

Still, no one in Wilton believed that our own man could possibly be defeated, and we went joyously to hear the poll declared. We were given a good and safe place, with Reggie and Beatrix Herbert, the children of the Conservative candidate, in a first-floor window facing the Town Hall, and overlooking the crowd. The counting went on for hours, but they were most enjoyable ones, spent in watching the ever-moving, ever-amusing crowd. Very few Liberals could be seen, and those few were good-humouredly chaffed and jostled by their opponents who, as they looked about them, could have no doubt that they were in a majority. But as time went on, grave faces appeared at the windows of the Town Hall, and secret signs were passed down to friends below. Conservatives who were 'in the know'

B

[33]

looked glum, but their glumness did not reach the rank-and-file, which included ourselves.

At last the Poll was declared. Sir Thomas Grove was the first member for the southern division of Wiltshire. Surely no successful candidate was ever so received. He seemed not to have a single friend. He came to the window to make the customary speech. A roar of hooting and booing drowned everything he said. Then appeared the beaten candidate. Passionate cheers received him, and every word he spoke was heard with reverent attention—every word indeed, till he asked for a hearing for his opponent. That was too much. Wilton was resolved that Sir Thomas Grove should not speak in its market-place that morning. And more, he dared not set foot among the crowd, for madness had seized the respectable burgesses of the town. Middle-aged pillars of society became crazy. The Town Hall has only one entrance, and round this there now pressed the whole population of the place, thirsting for the blood of the stranger who had presumed to think he would represent them in Parliament. Things looked ugly, and the Chief Constable telegraphed to Salisbury for reinforcements. After a time there appeared a contingent of seventy additional police. From our window we watched while this regiment formed up round the door of the Town Hall, and our new member was passed out from the shelter of the building, to be inserted into the middle of his bodyguard. Then they set off to march him to the railway station, for there were then no motors to carry him quickly out of reach, and horses would have been stopped by the crowd. Even so, it was not too easy. As the procession moved off, everyone in the market-place followed it with a rush. We ran from our window. and sped along behind. The crowd hurled itself upon the file of policemen, by sheer weight throwing it now this way, now that. The maddest man of all was George Carse, a magnificent figure of over six feet in height, His stately form and greying beard were well known to us all, for he handed the bag in church and appeared on ceremonial occasions in his councillor's robe, as he was before long to become Mayor of Wilton. Now, with his great strength and reach, he succeeded in breaking through the police cordon. He seized our un-happy member by the collar and gave him a good shake. For a moment it looked as if Sir Thomas must be throttled. Then the police turned upon Carse, whose huge figure was sent flying over the palings into the gardens of the Pembroke Arms, and the member was then successfully shepherded to the station and put into the train. He never came back to Wilton, preferring those parts of his constituency where interest in politics was less acute.

Yet we did have our torchlight procession that night. The torches were ready, and it would have been a pity to waste them. Moreover, everyone needed cheering, and what could be more cheering than they? So the town marched *en masse* to Wilton House, the torches crowding together in the courtyard, shining along the walls and glittering upon the windows. Speeches were made. Songs were sung. Like Old Sarum before it, Wilton had ceased to return a member of its own to the parliament of its country, and it had made its protest.

My memories of these early processions might well end with Queen Victoria's Jubilee, when, to my surprise and delight, I found myself for the first time seeing how they did these things in London. Our Mayor went to London to see the Queen keep her Jubilee, so our Wilton festivities were on the day before. That afternoon, as I was proudly presiding at one of the tables at the children's tea in the market-place, my father unexpectedly appeared, and, as I wrote in my diary, 'hauled me off to London'. I afterwards learnt that there had been prolonged discussion as to whether or not I was too young to go; and it had at last been decided that the younger the spectator, the longer she was likely to live to remember the occasion. This tipped the scales in my favour.

My father ordered me to write a diary of those days, and I still possess it. It was detailed, but dull, yet its very uninspired narrative still evokes for myself the memory of my reactions to that Jubilee Day. Our seats were on the House of Lords stand, outside St. Margaret's church, and when we reached them at eight o'clock in the morning, the route which lay before us was still so packed with carriages that I thought the procession would never be able to get through. But by ten o'clock it was clear, and a double row of red-coated soldiers showed plainly where the Queen was to come. Very soon after this, we heard the sound of cheering from Whitehall. It had begun, and sooner than we had expected. We sat eagerly forward to see come round the corner—a jolly old cockney workman driving a water-cart, for London streets were dusty in those days.

The whole crowd roared cheers and chaff at this absurd figure, who was not at all embarrassed by the ovation he received. He came down the route, bowing on both sides, and waving his hand. He was immensely enjoying himself. Nothing could have been grander than the spectacle itself, but there was still room on the day for this friendly little episode.

The water-cart was followed by a succession of dazzling sights. Three processions in all went to the Abbey that morning, and the first one consisted of Indian Princes driving in open landaus. As I read my diary, I see again their dresses and turbans 'made of glorious silks and satins of all colours, and covered with diamonds and all sorts of precious stones'. Some of them, I said, 'seemed to be a blaze of diamonds', and the obvious phrase does indeed recall to me the gasp of wonder with which one met the glare of those magnificent jewels burning in the sunlight of that wonderful June day. I can still see the dark proud mysterious faces of the princes, and their black beards.

A little pause, and then came the second procession, which I now feel sure must have been the most beautiful of all, although at the time I liked it least. In it came one after the other a succession of the gilt and painted state coaches from the royal stables; their four horses were harnessed with elaborate and most decorative trappings, and were driven by coachmen in eighteenth-century liveries, while royal footmen held the heads of every horse. In these coaches drove the European sovereigns who were attending the Jubilee, and to my regret I remarked that the coaches hid their faces. I did say, however, that 'in the distance, the state coaches looked lovely, like a picture of hundreds of years ago'.

The queen drove in the last procession, surrounded by a mounted bodyguard of her sons and grandsons, and preceded by the English princesses in carriages. I tried with all my might to write down my personal impressions of each of these, though I lamented that they went by too quickly for me to see them properly. I thought the Duke of Connaught 'very good-looking', and the Duchess of Albany 'very popular', while Princess Maud was 'a dear little thing with a dear little tiny face'. The Prince of Wales looked 'very jolly' as he rode on 'a splendid horse' directly in front of the Queen, with the Dukes of Edinburgh and of Connaught on either hand; but I declared that 'the most kingly man of all' was the Crown Prince of Germany in his shining white uniform.

As the Queen drove to the Abbey, I was disappointed because she did not look up as she passed us, and I thought that her face was 'very pale and sad'; but as she came back 'she looked quite happy and smiled and bowed'. In fact, I added kindly, 'she looked very nice indeed'.

I must have been a funny little girl, for I see by my diary that, except for the jewels of the Indian Princes, the gorgeous pageantry of the day did not much impress me. What I was looking for was the intimate expression on the faces of the people who drove by. I wanted to know what they were like. It was this which interested me.

The procession of Indian Princes was the last to

leave the Abbey and we got off our stand and walked
round to the West Door to see those glorious men get
into their carriages. I enjoyed this close view of the
jewels I had so much admired in the morning, but
again, our easy approach to the Abbey door shows
how simple the arrangements must then have been.
People could move about the route with very little
difficulty. Before we left our stand, we had seen the
Bishop of London come out of the Abbey where he
had been officiating, tuck up his robes, and run some
way down the route to a stand where a seat was waiting
for him. He did not heed the laughter and the cheers
of the crowd who welcomed him as they had welcomed
the dustman in the morning. He meant to see the procession.

When we reached Wilton next day, my sister Mildred
had a sad story to tell. An important part of the Wilton
Jubilee celebrations had been a dinner in the market-
place, when the whole grown-up population of the
town had sat down to feast off steaming roast beef and
'viggety pudden', as the Wiltshire people call plum
pudding. In the evening, when we had gone to London, Mildred had found a rather feeble-minded young
labourer crying his heart out in his mother's wash-
house, because he had lost his ticket, and so had been
shut out of the banquet. Mildred implored my father
to do something about it, and the young man was
accordingly sent one of the lavish meals which had
been provided for invalids and old people who could
not walk to the market-place. But it was no good. The
boy shook his head and pushed away the plate. He

could not eat. Indeed he did not want to. He was not crying for roast beef and plum pudding, but for having missed the fun of eating them in the market-place with the sun shining down upon his head.

II

* ECONOMIES *

We sometimes think of the later Victorian and the
Edwardian times as days of care-free opulence, when
everyone was rich and secure, and when neither individuals nor nations knew what it meant to stand on
the brink of bankruptcy. In a way this is true. Incomes
seemed to be safe and secure when I was a child. Young
people married possessing either a large or a small fortune invested in 'the Funds', and they knew just what
that fortune was. Every year 'the Funds' produced the
same income upon the investments. To this solid permanent foundation, professional men added the steadily
rising incomes derived from their professions; and they
were confident that as their families grew, their resources were bound to grow correspondingly.

Yet that old prosperity rested upon a background of
frugality unattempted to-day, although everyone com-
plains of poverty, a thing which nobody used to do. It
was considered bad form to talk about money, whether
to say you had too much or too little of it. You were
expected to live up to your position and under your
income, and to say nothing about it: you tacitly kept

a watchful eye on your bankbook to make sure that
this precise balance was always maintained.

My father was a country parson with a large house
and a small living, and he had ten children. He also
had a great sense of ecclesiastical dignity. The population of Wilton with its little hamlet of Netherhampton
was about two thousand. There were two churches
and two curates. Nowadays this would be an excessive
staff, especially as my father hardly ever left home even
for a day. But in his eyes it was essential that at least
two clergymen should always be present at the Sunday
services in Wilton church, he thought a solitary parson
so inadequate as to be almost ridiculous there. He was
extremely active in mind as well as in body, and he was
for ever thinking of new mediums for Church work,
all of which cost money; and yet he was determined
that the old things should always be done in the old
opulent way, however many new things arose to be
paid for too. Nothing would induce him to cut the cas-
sock according to the cloth. So it came about that most
of the small acounts published annually in the parish
magazine ended with the words: '*Balance paid by Rector.*'

Then there were the expenses of his family and
household, by no means small ones. Although there
was no bathroom at the Rectory, everyone had as many
baths as they do to-day, taking them, however, in tubs
in the privacy of their own rooms. My father was
revolted by the idea of people meeting and passing on
the threshold of a bathroom, or of anyone's stepping
into a bath just vacated by someone else. Such things
were not tolerated under his roof. Extra baths had

therefore to mean extra work, and we had a constant succession of under-housemaids, nursery-maids, and between-maids, whose chief work was to carry cans of water upstairs. A dim background was built up of charwomen doing the 'heavy work'—raking out stoves, or scrubbing passages and back stairs.

At one time, six of my brothers were simultaneously at public schools, which must have meant an enormous annual expense; but in spite of these fresh calls on their income, my parents continued to live in the style of their parents before them—formal dinners, with a good many courses, and two waitresses if the number of diners was more than three. My father was an ascetic man with a small appetite, and the length of a dinner was for him purely a matter of decency and good manners. For instance, when one of his friends sent him a present of game, he would never allow it to be treated as a main course. Game had always to appear as an extra following the joint. I remember the pained surprise with which I once heard him say to my mother: 'Is *this* our dinner?', when she once broke this rule and allowed a brace of pheasants to be served as the *pièce de résistance*. What was in my father's mind was this. He would not live on his friends, and they would not expect him to do so. Their presents were enjoyable bonnes-bouches: nothing more. In those days no decent people bought game in shops. Owners of shooting did not sell their game, but gave it away in lavish presents to their friends; and it was generally believed that bought game had been killed by poachers, so that its buying ought to be discouraged.

When I remember the number of joints which hung in the larder at Wilton Rectory; and the huge unpacking when 'the stores' arrived—tin canisters and earthenware jars of sugar, coffee, cocoa-nibs, tea, rice, raisins, sultanas and prunes—I see that our establishment was run on a scale unknown in the country rectories of to-day. Yet this lavishness was accompanied by economies even more unknown.

In the last decades of the nineteenth century, there was of course no central heating at Wilton Rectory; but the hall, the passages, and the wide upstair corridor were all warmed by a huge, hideous, and miraculously effective stove which stood foresquare in the middle of the hall. It was taken away in the summer, and however cold the autumn might be, it never reappeared until after the Confirmation in the middle of November. There was a good reason for this. The Bishop robed in the study, and from there he always began his ceremonial procession to the church, my father marching before him, clad too in his robes, and carrying the Pastoral Staff. Bishop Wordsworth was built on a large scale, and it would have been impossible, with any safety, to manœuvre the vast expanse of surplice and lawn sleeves round the often red-hot stove, so we shivered till the Bishop had paid his visit.

After that, the blacksmith carried in the elephantine black monstrosity, and planted it in the middle of the hall, its long chimney being carried horizontally to a hole in the wall over the door which led to the kitchen regions. From that moment till the end of the winter, the house was bathed in the soft diffused warmth which spread from the stove in all directions. Except for its appearance, it was the best stove I ever knew, but now-adays no house-proud family would tolerate such a hideosity in their midst.

Not one ounce of fuel was ever bought to feed the stove. The ashes from all the grates in the house were collected to be carefully sieved by the garden-boy in the back yard. He threw them against an upright sieve which looked like an easel. The fine dust made the kit-chen garden path, and the large cinders were burnt in the stove. Nothing else. In fact the stove shared the economical standards of the day. It refused to burn anything but those old ashes. If a housemaid hoped to start it more quickly in the morning by beginning it with a shovelful of coal, the stove at once 'clinkered up' and went out, and all the world knew what she had done. Never was there a more cosy, more permeating, or more effective system of heating.

There was no electric light in Wilton, and when we moved from room to room, we carried our oil lamps with us. A characteristic memory of my father is the sight of him coming from the study, carrying a lamp through the hall to the drawing-room, or leading the way in to dinner with a lamp in his hand, to be placed on the sideboard for the parlour-maid's use. Candles burnt on the dining-room table, and in the bedrooms only candles were used, so at sundown a row of flat silver bedroom candlesticks was placed on a small cabinet in the hall. These were carried by anyone who went up-stairs after dark. A box of matches stood beside the candlesticks; and indeed, as is the case to-day, matches were to be seen on the tables in every room, though they were not then used for lighting cigarettes. Smoking was only allowed in the room which had been the schoolroom, and which was well out of the way; though when the servants were safely in bed, my father and his male guests used to perambulate to the Servants' Hall where they smoked in secrecy for an hour or two.

Matches in the sitting-rooms were meant only for lighting candles and for sealing letters; and as soon as the winter fires were lit, the matchboxes were moved into the background, and in front of each was placed a vase ('vause' my father called it) containing paper spills. How near we then were to the poetry of life! A girl lighting her candle with a spill, lit from a stove in which burnt the ashes of last winter's fires, was in the tradition of the Vestal Virgins: while the man who carried the light to his pipe from the fire in his grate, was of the family of Prometheus.

Then there were economies in journeys. To begin with, their number was limited. Travelling by train now costs if anything rather more than it did before the war, but it was then looked upon as quite an exceptional expense. Country people did not think of running up to London every week, or of staying in a different house every week-end. Many engagements were fitted into one journey. When I once developed an alarming cough, and was taken to London to see a specialist, my mother and I left Wilton station at half-past seven on a winter morning, so that we might get full value for our tickets, as we should thus have time to see not only the doctor, but the National

Gallery and the South Kensington Museum as well.

People stayed in each other's houses more seldom, but when they came, they stayed longer. They 'saved their pockets' by making a round of visits arranged on an elaborate plan worked out with the help of Bradshaw. Many visits lasted a week or a fortnight, and some of my uncles and aunts always came for a month every summer.

When our guests arrived, only very honoured or very lame ones were met at the station by a cab. Everyone else was escorted on foot, to and from the station by a large or small contingent of the family, their luggage being brought to the house in the donkey-cart, or pushed by the garden-boy in a wheelbarrow or a pair of trucks. Those walks to and from the station helped to keep us and our guests on easy terms with the townspeople. Everybody knew who had come to stay. When my sister came home for the first time after her marriage, we, most of us, met her at the station, and a jolly old dame called out as we passed her house:

'Any family, Mrs. Collins?'

'Not yet.'

'Never mind. If at first you don't succeed, try, try, try again.'

These friendly greetings cannot reach a passing motor car.

I remember one funny little economy which I am sure has been now outgrown by even the most old-fashioned of nannies. When we learnt to sew, our nurse would place the hem or seam for us, and then tack it. When we had laboriously and clumsily crawled down our piece of work with the needle, we were taught to draw out the tacking thread, and wind it upon an empty reel. It was then used again and again.

Perhaps cotton was very expensive in those days, for when my mother gave out garments and children's clothes to be made before Christmas by poor seamstresses out of work, she always gave them too the cotton to sew with. But no one was given a whole reel. It was our part as children to wind off on little twists of paper the quantity allotted for each garment, and this allowance, and no more, was given away with the material.

Paper and string were, of course, carefully saved from all parcels which came to the house, and the string was made into neat loops and kept in a drawer in the dining-room. In an adjoining drawer were placed the half-sheets of unused notepaper, torn from the backs of letters. We played an enormous number of word games at Wilton, and these were written on the large sheets of paper which had contained parcels from the grocer. To this day, the mention of certain games calls up for me the faint far-distant aroma of Mr. Gidding's brand of China tea, and I see again the very pretty early nineteenth-century trade advertisement which was printed in pale red ink on the paper which he used for packing his most homely parcels.

Sending the boys to school was a costly business, and so for a long time there was no governess for the 'little girls'. Our 'education' would be despised to-day. My mother taught us herself. We learnt everything by heart—pieces of poetry, passages from the Bible, history, geography, or French and Latin grammar; and then she came to us for about half an hour to 'hear us'. After that she wrote copies for us, in her lovely harmonious handwriting, leaving us by ourselves writing for an hour or so. I only had lessons from real governesses for four years of my life, and money was certainly saved on the education of my sisters and me, but though our training was very unconventional, I think we were not any the worse for that. We learnt how to read for ourselves, in English and in French, and were given plenty of opportunity to do both. We learnt how to live in the family circle, which costs nothing, and is very useful in after life.

As children we were abominably dressed. This was of course partly from economy, though it must also be confessed that my mother was completely destitute of dress-sense. She was indeed in many ways blind to appearances. Her humorously affectionate vision saw chiefly what was beneath the surface. She did appreciate my father's good looks, but as for her children, she loved them equally whatever their appearance. She did not care what we looked like. In fact she did not know. Mildred and I once stood on the platform at Wilton station, watching my parents starting for a flower show. My father turned and said something to Mamma. We read the words on his lips.

'Let us take the little girls.'

She at once agreed, and came to the window to call us. Then we saw him say something else. It was this.

'No. We can't. They are too untidy.'

I still feel the humiliation, but I am sure he was right.

We probably looked complete ragamuffins, but my
mother would never have seen it. Nor did she remember the episode afterwards. It was not the kind of thing
she would think of again, though I do once remember
her being most indignant when Gertrude Lady Pembroke said to her with affectionate mockery.

'Dear Mrs. O., Always so nice and shabby.'

My father dressed well, and wanted his wife to do so
too. He once looked at her rather critically, aware that
something was wrong, and wondering what could be
done about it.

'That dress does not look right. It wants *something*.
Perhaps a knot of cherry-coloured ribbon?'

The cherry-coloured ribbon became a family saying,
but something more than that was wanted to make my
mother 'look right'.

WITHOUT KNOWING MR. WALKLEY

III

★ PEOPLE I HAVE FORGOTTEN ★

Nowadays, one meets fewer 'Characters' than of old, and life seems to be far more uniform. Everyone knew some oddities in their childhood, curious people who looked and behaved quite unlike others, but such pronounced individuality is rare to-day. Forty or fifty years ago, the streets of Wilton teemed with odd personalities, but to-day they seem to have disappeared. Unfortunately, some of the most striking of these figures are so far away that they only swim faintly on the misty horizon of my memory. I wish I could remember them better.

I half recall the form of Old Stroud, the cabinet maker, who must have been as delicate a craftsman as Chippendale himself, though without the masterly invention of that great man. Stroud had a large flat gentle face, surrounded by a thin Newgate fringe of pale brown hair. He stammered badly, and his eyes looked sorrowfully out as he vainly tried to enunciate his words. I know not whether he was the founder of the firm which bears his name in Wilton, but he was bent on his sons carrying it on, so much so that his dying words were:

'Walter to make the coffin.' No rival undertaker should intervene upon this family prerogative.

Then there was Mr. Savage, the Prior of the little Hospital of St. John of Jerusalem at the end of the street. His voice was that of a very noisy raven; and he could also make a gigantic click with his tongue when he was encouraging the paces of the tandem donkeys which he always drove in an enormous and luxuriously padded Bath chair. This noise of his could be heard a quarter of a mile away, and it meant that the racing tandem would shortly rush round the corner, with Mr. Savage standing up in the Bath chair waving the reins and cheering on his donkeys. He taught his dog to run to the railway embankment to pick up the newspaper which the guard always threw out for him from the morning express train from London; and he always declared that when one morning the *Chronicle* was thrown out by mistake instead of the *Standard*, the dog spat it out, and refused to bring home this Liberal Rag. Mr. Savage was a *bon viveur*, and possessed, like other clerics of his day, a celebrated cellar. When he was at last dying from dropsy, and lay, looking very miserable, all the fun and humour gone from his face, the doctor proposed to relieve him by drawing off some of the fluid which was creeping up round his heart. He dolefully refused.

'Nothing that's been tapped lasts long in this house,' he said.

In those long-ago days, I sometimes heard my father say: 'This bread is not very good.' To which my mother would reply: 'We shall have the new flour in a week or two.' Or he said: 'What good bread!' and then she answered: 'It's the new flour.'

Those phrases marked an epoch, though my parents would have been surprised to hear it. People never do know which of their everyday habits or sayings will surprise their successors; and this one meant that the flour we used was grown and milled in the neighbourhood, and that the bread we ate was made in the house. Made, but not baked: and this brings me to another half-forgotten figure—George Street. I wish I had known him better. He was a tall yellow-haired man with a long slouching tread, and he came to the Rectory on Wednesdays and Saturdays to carry off the dough kneaded by the cook, in order to bake it in his brick oven. He plunged his arms into the great earthenware pot which stood by the kitchen fire, and swung the ball of dough into a sack, which he then threw over his shoulder and strode away, looking like the picture in *Reading without Tears* of:

P is like a man with a Pack on his back.

He seldom spoke to us, but in spite of this, we were all fascinated by him, for he had a surly independent charm. Too charming, he must have been, for he got into one of those scrapes which then were not discussed before the children, and he left Wilton early, under a cloud.

A very different type was old Thresher, who had no charm at all, but was a completely farcical figure. He was a narrow old man, with a long thin straggling grey beard, and he was generally seen bustling about with a black cotton sack in his hand. His appearance was simply absurd, but really he was a most sinister person. He was a miser. He kept a tiny shop almost opposite the Rectory, and indeed it had to be small, as all its stock-in-trade was carried into it, in relays, by old Thresher himself, in that black cotton sack. He was too stingy to part with enough money at any one time to buy his goods wholesale: he preferred to spend a few shillings at a time in the Salisbury shops. He would not afford a railway ticket for the journey to Salisbury, nor would he pay the carrier to bring his stock to Wilton. So he walked the three miles to Salisbury two or three times each week, with the empty sack under his arm; and a few hours later he walked home—his brisk one-sided tread a little less brisk and a little more one-sided, while the sack, now very bulgy, hung from his hand.

In Salisbury, Mr. Thresher had of course paid the usual retail prices for his goods, and in Wilton he sold them for twice those amounts, or more. It was odd that he found customers. Probably it was sometimes convenient for Wilton people to buy a reel of cotton or a piece of tape near home; and by the sale of trifles like these, Thresher slowly built up quite a little fortune. He invested his savings in derelict house property which he let to very poor people who could not complain of the condition of their cottages, as they could not afford to move out of them. He went from house to house collecting his rents on the days when he did not walk to Salisbury.

Mrs. and Miss Thresher sold in the shop, and we

were often their customers. Our favourite purchases were halfpenny balls of wool. In Salisbury Mr. Thresher bought skeins of very cheap wool in bright colours, and then he and his wife and daughter wound this off into balls containing each about a yard. These were just what we wanted for making our Christmas presents We made woollen balls for babies by twisting our wool round two cardboard circles, and then clipping the edges; or else we made wool mats in French knitting. This horrible craft is, I hope, now forgotten, for nothing could be more ugly than it is. Its one charm was that it was extremely easy to do. Four tintacks were hammered into an empty cotton reel, and a succession of loops twisted over these. Then a long wormlike thing began to ooze out from the opposite end of the reel. We French knitted short lengths of wool of every colour, and finally twisted the variegated worm into a round wool mat to be presented to a mother or some other grown-up female relation.

For children, the most attractive corner in Thresher's shop was the penny window—a narrow slit of glass in which were displayed the delapidated toys which the old man bought up for next to nothing, so that even at a penny each they brought him in a handsome profit. Children's noses were always pressed against this window; and never in my life have I wanted anything more than a most clumsily made Toby jug of some sort of stoneware which once lay there. On it was the face of a bearded nigger, quite hideous, and moulded very roughly. I was bent on possessing it, and though my mother was not in favour of it, she allowed me to buy it at last. For a week I was supremely happy. It really was as delightful as I expected. Then one day, I used it to hold painting water, and I washed it afterwards. When it came out of the wash-tub, the nigger was a nigger no more. His face was a dead white, upon which the lumps and excrescences which had been so fascinating in the negroid type had become only deformities. My one wish was that Mamma should never see this metamorphosis. It would have too cruelly proved that she had been right. I felt this very much.

The townspeople said of Mr. Thresher that he attended either Church or Chapel without prejudice in favour of either, as long as he was always present for the collection. This was not from generosity. He wanted to hand the bag. As he had customers of all denominations, he was determined to be seen by all in whatever place of worship he was present.

He added to his income in all sorts of ways—by waiting at the Mayor's banquet, or at my father's annual choir supper. After one of these he won a nickname which stuck to him for life—Old Apple-Pie. It somehow became known that he had carried home as perquisites an uneaten apple tart and a rice pudding, and a few evenings later, an anonymous rhymed alphabet was pushed under the door of every house in the town. It began:

> *A was an Apple-Pie made for the choir.*
> *B was the Baker who baked it with fire.*
> *C was the Cook who made it look nice.*
> *D was the Draper who liked it with rice.*

I believe the waggish poet was never identified.

Deaf old Mrs. Staples lived a few doors away from Thresher. She was the wife of the chemist. Beside her cheeks were unchangingly set some bunches of very hard, neat, grey curls, and she wore a large frilled cap trimmed with bows of magenta ribbon. Cairngorms were her favourite stones, and the high tucker of starched lace at her throat was always fastened by a very large one. When a customer rang the bell, Mr. Staples would shuffle rather furtively into the shop from the sitting-room, taking care to shut the glass door behind him. In spite of this, it was always possible to hear the loud unmodulated deaf voice of Mrs. Staples, talking angrily about Predestination with her friends.

'We know that the Childurn of Israel were chosen from all Eternity to be the Elect of Jehovah,' she chanted triumphantly, though I know not why this gave her such immense personal delight; but how I should now have enjoyed these tremendous conversations!

In those days, Wilton post office was simply one of the ordinary small houses in the Square, and it must have been very difficult for strangers to find it. You opened the door upon a lobby measuring about two feet square, on one side of which was a window of frosted glass. The customer tapped upon this, and then it flew up with a snap to reveal the cross face of Miss Young, the postmistress. She seemed to be overcome with rage if anyone dared to buy a stamp from her, and we were terrified of her. She did, however, once unbend sufficiently to teach my mother how to open an envelope so cunningly that no one could possibly guess that it had been touched. A useful art for a postmistress.

Wandering about the roads and lanes of Wiltshire, it has always been possible to come across specimens of that charming if quarrelsome race—the race of born Antiquaries. The Wiltshire strain begins in the seventeenth century with Aubrey, the most winning of gossips. He soon escaped from his tutors, whom he thought 'dull, ignorant, rest-in-the-house teachers', and spent his life among 'umbrages, Osney House ruins, etc., and antiquities'. He finished nothing, but he filled a number of pocket-books with 'philosophical and antiquarian remarks' for his own amusement and the delight of his friends. Thus, 'by God's Providence', as he said, he found happiness, though 'his businesses and affaires ran kim-kam', and he lost all his money. More than two hundred years later, Sir Richard Colt Hoare was still at it, but in a more systematic way, for he published the result of his researches in some huge tomes which no Wiltshire historians can yet do without. He dug and measured and wrote things down, though unfortunately his company was so agreeable that he was often detained too long over luncheon with the local squire during his excavations. He left his labourers to go on with the digging and only strolled out late in the afternoon to see what they had thought worth saving among their finds.

Two Antiquaries of the old school were living in Wilton when I was a child, and they died within a few months of each other, some time in the early 'nineties. Like Aubrey, Mr. Nightingale and Mr. Swayne wrote very little down, and most of their learning perished with them. My father constantly quoted bits of old Wiltshire knowledge on no authority but the word of one of these two, and they must have made the most delightful companions. Each of them loved the county with a love resembling that of an old family servant, and the past of Wiltshire lay in their minds as if it were their own. They were chain-talkers too, a reference to one thing evoking from them a flow of associated memories.

Mr. Swayne was also a chain-smoker, with a cigar always in his mouth and a book in his hand. He built an enormous library (since pulled down) on to his house, the Island, at Wilton, but its walls could never hold his books. They lay in heaps on the floor, jumbled up with cigar boxes empty and full, till his son succeeded him and spent several years in tidying up the litter.

Mr. Swayne was a tall thin handsome man with a sardonic expression, and a gift for sarcastic epigram which was said (with what truth I know not) to have lost him half a fortune. In his youth he had been a barrister, and the story goes that once he shot one of the poisoned shafts of his wit across the Court at the sitting judge, who happened to be his own father, and who at once went home and altered his will.

Mr. Swayne was 'an old man who wouldn't say his prayers' except at three o'clock on Sunday afternoons, so, while he lived, a special Evensong was always said in Wilton church for his benefit at this hour. From our nursery window, we always saw him pass on his way to this service, with Mrs. Swayne, a small round woman, walking a few steps behind him.

The Swaynes had several daughters, one of whom was of so dazzling a beauty that she was a legend in her lifetime, and the old ladies at the parties in the Bishop's palace at Salisbury used to cluster round the door to see her come in. The whole county was in love with her, though she was only nineteen when she married a most brilliant barrister much older than herself. In less than a year, he had a complete and permanent breakdown, and this lovely creature returned to Wilton to live in a tiny house in the Square with her baby daughter. She was like her father, a curious aloof character, and now she became very much a recluse. Only three or four special friends were ever admitted to her house, their names being inscribed on a list hung in the hall, so that the parlour-maid might refresh her memory on her way to answer the bell. My eldest sister was one of the chosen.

Mr. Nightingale's personality was of another quality to that of Mr. Swayne, with its bitter tang and its touch of mockery. The Nightingales were well known in the county as wine-merchants, though I never heard of Mr. Nightingale selling a bottle of wine. However, as his affairs did not 'run kim-kam', and he lived in comfortable leisure to the end of his life, I presume that other members of his family carried on the business, while he lived peacefully with his sister at the Mount. The walls of two of the rooms in this house were glazed to secure the remains of what had been a unique collection of early English porcelain; and here Mr. Nightingale was often to be found, his quiet face very serene, and his calm brown eyes resting affectionately upon some specially loved 'piece' which he happened to be showing to one of his friends. He loved his china as an old man might love an exquisite young girl living in his house, in whom he sees—behind her own beauty—another beauty, long vanished from his sight. And something of this belonged to Mr. Nightingale's China Room, for in it, this calm selfless man was in the presence of the sorrow of his life. The collection was only a part of what he once had possessed. The most beautiful of his specimens, the rarest, those which had meant for him those magic moments in a collector's life when he knows that he has found his pearl of great price—most of these had been destroyed in a fire at the Alexandra Palace. He had lent the best of his possessions for an exhibition there. Mr. Nightingale did not look like a broken-hearted man, yet this was a loss from which he never recovered.

Mr. Nightingale had other tastes than china. He loved by-ways in art, and generally quiet-coloured things. This quality appealed to him first of all in his porcelain, but it was seen again in his medieval needlework, and his portfolios of reproductions of Italian Primitifs. Ancient seals, Gothic stained glass, Church Plate—in all of these he was deeply learned; and as a younger man he had travelled extensively and stored his retentive memory with the works of Byzantine, Renaissance, and Romanesque art. Those things remained in his mind, in his little house which bordered upon the fairground at Wilton; and living there in the presence of so much august beauty and splendour, he remained the most modest and unassuming of men.

While he moved mentally in happy intimacy among the Stones of Venice and of Stonehenge, he outwardly stayed content in his garden, behind the gigantic wall of box and yew which concealed it from the highroad.

IV

★ FAMILY PRAYERS ★

The first Lady Radnor whom I remember was a very remarkable woman, a fine musician and a convinced spiritualist. In those days there often stayed at Longford a Miss Wingfield who was clairvoyante, and she was one of the party at the marriage of the only daughter of the house to Lord Skelmersdale, Lord Lathom's son. Miss Wingfield arrived a day before the other guests, and that evening, when she was sitting alone with her host and hostess, it was suggested that she should gaze in the crystal for something connected with the wedding. She took the crystal, and the others waited. After a few moments she began to describe what seemed to be a most absurd picture, in no way connected with what was in all their minds.

'What *are* those people doing?' she asked. 'They seem to be *smelling their chairs*. What can that mean? Oh, I see now, this is family prayers, and those are the servants kneeling in a row. An old man with a long beard is reading. A lady is kneeling a little way off, and now she gets up from her knees, crosses to the old man, and whispers something to him. He waves her away, and she goes back to her place.'

That was all. It seemed very pointless. The next evening, Lord and Lady Lathom arrived, and Miss Wingfield at once recognized them as the two people she had seen in the crystal. Lady Radnor asked them whether they had family prayers on the previous night. They had.

'Did anyone move while they were going on?'

Then Lady Lathom said that during prayers, she had gone to Lord Lathom and had asked him to say a special prayer for the bride and bridegroom. He had silenced her with his hand, telling her that he had already decided to do so.

The point of this story here is that nowadays few people would recognize the chair-smelling scene as the ceremony of family prayers. The present generation hardly ever sees it, though for those of us who are relics of Queen Victoria's day, nothing more vividly recalls the atmosphere of duty and decorum in which we grew up. Great houses had their chapels and chaplains, and, early in the century, even their sermons. My father, who came to Wilton in the 'sixties as Chaplain to Lord and Lady Herbert of Lea, used to tell us that one Sunday evening, when Bishop Wilberforce was a guest in the house, he rose up at the end of prayers, and delivered one of those hour-long sermons to which the mid-Victorians were accustomed. At the harmonium sat Eddy Hamilton, an Eton friend of the sons of the house, waiting to play a final hymn. Like the young man who tired of St. Paul's sermon at Troas, Eddy too, after a time, 'sunk down with sleep'; but unluckily his elbows fell upon the keyboard and his feet upon the

bellows. A roar of discordant notes startled the congregation, and woke the sleeper; while the Bishop
probably thought he was being 'blowed down', like a
preacher in Salisbury Cathedral, who had once gone
on for two hours, and at last came to the end of the
patience of the organist.

In ordinary houses, family prayers did not rise to
the dignity of a sermon, although the master of the
house would sometimes expound from a commentary.
Prayers were generally said, not in a chapel, but in the
breakfast-room, and disrespectful people made play
with jokes about 'praying to the urn'. It is true that
an accompaniment of bubbling and boiling often made
a background for the voice; while a flustered member
of the family was sometimes seen rising hurriedly from
his or her knees, to blow out the light under a too
vigorously spitting kettle.

The routine was fixed. Chairs were placed in a row
for the servants, who marched into the room in strict
order of precedence. Generally they first sat on their
chairs for a Bible reading, and then they turned over to
'smell them'. The family knelt informally round about
the breakfast-table, ostensibly attending to the service,
but sometimes taking surreptitious peeps at the bundles
of letters which had been placed on the table before
each person's seat.

An old lady living in Wilton had been the heroine
of what must have been surely the one and only romance of family prayers. She had belonged to a large
family of sisters, living with a most severe parent
in Smith Square, Westminster. The sisters were all

heiresses, but such was in those days the standard of chaperonage, that none of them had ever found herself alone with a young man. Our old friend had at last collected a lover, but how could he propose? Privacy was impossible. This ingenious young man had the brilliant idea of proposing during family prayers, and we made many guesses as to how he achieved it.

My brother Harold decided that he responded fervently in the Litany.

'I beseech thee to have me good Laura.'

Laura was not her name, but doubtless the adored one was quick enough to glance demurely in her admirer's direction when she murmured her next AMEN.

Evening prayers were not general except in clerical houses, but even there they sometimes failed in their effect through being introduced too unexpectedly into the stream of common life. It was often a great shock at Wilton Rectory, when we were playing games after dinner, to see the door suddenly open to admit a swift procession which disposed itself discreetly on its knees before the chairs at the far end of the room. The parlour-maid detached herself from the others, and, approaching my father, she presented him with a book. Laughter was abruptly stilled. Conversation froze on the lips. Counters rolled from the card-table. Everyone flopped down to 'smell their chairs'. But it must be admitted that this swift turnover to devotion was too sudden for any but the most gymnastic minds.

It was the servants who usually took the family by surprise, but once, at any rate, in our house, the tables were turned. My father must have been bored with his evening, and looking at the clock, he saw that the servants were late for prayers. He rang the bell sharply. There was a pause. He rang again. This time the kitchen-maid appeared, covered with confusion, as the rule of the house was that the young maids should not appear at evening prayers. They were supposed to be in bed. Now this embarrassed girl had to report that the upper servants were 'having a game' and were all dressed up, so they couldn't possibly appear. They were not let off. A grave message was sent, ordering them to change, and to appear in ten minutes. Exactly at that moment, the door opened, and the customary procession entered. The carriage of the maids was perfect. Their figures stiff and rigid in the firm stays which controlled their panting: the parlour-maid handed the Prayer Book without meeting my father's eyes: he took it with his usual gravity; and then all the flushed and guilty faces were comfortably buried in the chair seats. Only when Mildred and I were having our hair brushed upstairs did we learn that our respectable maids had actually been dressed as men, and had *worn trousers*—whose, we never learnt.

My first dinner party was at the palace at Salisbury in the days of Bishop Wordsworth. Most of the guests were old and very dignified, but there was one young man of my own age, Algy Bathurst. After dinner, he and I withdrew to a distant corner for a little light conversation, when all at once we caught sight of the last of the other guests disappearing through the drawing-room door. We had been left isolated. Horrified at the idea of doing the wrong thing, we followed at full speed, only to catch sight of that same figure vanishing through yet another door. We followed. Inside stood an unsmiling chaplain, who gravely motioned us in opposite directions. We did as we were told and then at once we found ourselves face to face in choir stalls on either side of a chapel. Before we had had time to pull ourselves together, yet another chaplain had begun to read compline. I have never forgotten the shock of that unprepared *volte-face*.

Family prayers are nowadays not easy to arrange because the routine of our days is so unlike that of the last century. It would be truer to say that our days have no routine. But in Queen Victoria's time, country life was very regular, and we did not sit lightly in our places. We were glued in. Day followed day in an admired regularity. My parents were really annoyed even to hear of people moving rapidly and frequently (in the then meaning of those words) from one place to another. Most people stayed at home, except for certain regularly planned visits, which were generally as annual as Christmas Day, and were always arranged weeks, or even months ahead. No one appeared unexpectedly from motors or aeroplanes. And the whole household fell into this steady round. Servants were engaged as under-housemaids, nursery-maids, or kitchen-maids, and moved slowly up to the higher grades. If they 'left to be married', it was only after a courtship lasting two or three years at least. Meals were always at the same hours, and nobody was ever late. Everyone came down to breakfast. Not to do so would interfere with the routine of the whole house. In one house in

Dorset where I stayed every year with my parents, the party assembled in the drawing-room before breakfast, to move from there to the breakfast-room in strict order of precedence, when the butler had flung open the door to announce that 'Breakfast is served, Sir Richard'.

Before this, our host had read prayers in the hall, and from his place, he fortunately could not see the staircase, upon which belated guests would perch themselves at different heights. As the servants were filing out, a covey of figures fluttered up from these various levels, trying to give the impression that they were all rising from their knees on the floor of the hall.

A hostess of course never stayed in her room for a meal except during her confinements, and these were carried out with the same unfailing regularity as were all other engagements in this completely planned life.

Nowadays, both guests and servants are always going and coming, and it is almost impossible to arrest their rapid flight for long enough to invite them to family prayers. Also, people's servants are too often paid strangers, rather than family friends, and with them most people would be too shy to suggest praying. Sometimes this cowardice is misplaced. In Bishop Donaldson's drawing-room at Salisbury a year or two before his death, there was one day a conversation about family prayers. The Bishop asked if many people still had them, and nearly everyone said 'No'. Mrs. Buckley was one of the exceptions, and she said that one of her reasons for keeping up the practice was that her servants liked it so much.

'In fact,' she went on, 'it's all I can do to prevent my guests from coming too.'

'*Prevent* them from coming?' asked the Bishop, astounded.

'Of course. They would make me far too shy.'

Everybody laughed, but she was quite right. Reading prayers is a very frightening thing. I am used to reading aloud, and I like doing it. In fact I often compel the guests in my house to listen while I indulge in this pastime. But when I have once or twice found myself on my knees, reading collects which are quite familiar to me and are quite easy to read, then a most extraordinary tremor comes into my voice. It floats up and down to an accompaniment of little sobs which nothing can control. I remember being suddenly called upon to read prayers when my mother was ill, when my voice sounded so exactly as if I was crying, that the servants left the room in tears too, thinking that I must have heard the invalid's death warrant. After that, I often read prayers when my parents were ill, but I never allowed even my sister to hear me doing so.

After the war, when the Women's Land Army was being dissolved, I was present at an evening service on its last Sunday, at one of our Wiltshire hostels. It was read by a welfare officer in charge, and as we began, she turned to me and said:

'You will give a Blessing at the end, won't you?'

There was no time to say no. The service had begun, and never shall I forget how my heart beat through those seemingly interminable prayers. Fortunately I have a good memory for hymns, and a very short one came into my mind. When the moment came, I faltered out No. 551 in Hymns, Ancient and Modern. Everyone in the room had often sung it, but they failed to recognize it when they heard it spoken; and they thought my 'Blessing' was a completely original inspiration.

My aunt, Amy Eden, who always seemed able to meet any situation, sympathized with and shared this panic. She told me that she was once called upon to read prayers at Eden Court when my grandfather and his chaplain were both out. She got on well till the last prayer of all, when she saw, printed before her:

'*The Grace of our Lord, etc.*'

She read those five words aloud, and then her mind became a blank. She stared speechless, through what seemed an endless pause. At last a voice rose up from that part of the room where the servants were patiently 'smelling their chairs', and the little prayer was finished by James, my grandfather's old servant.

Of course he should have been chosen from the first to be the deputy chaplain, for he was extremely episcopal. I only once remember my grandfather's staying at Wilton, for I was not very old when he died; but when Grandpapa and James arrived together, we were much confused. We knew that one of them was a bishop, and we could not imagine which. Grandpapa was very gay and lighthearted, while James was unfailingly solemn, and we decided that it must be he. So when one day my father found my small brother in the hall and asked: 'Where's the Bishop?', Harold promptly answered: 'In the pantry.'

Every Monday morning, at Wilton Rectory, the final collect at family prayers was the one I liked best in the week. This is how I heard it.

'*The sisters* mercifully O Lord, in these our supplications and prayers. And dispose the way of Thy servants toward the attainment of everlasting salvation; that, among all the changes and chances of this mortal life, they may ever be defended by Thy most gracious and ready help; through Jesus Christ our Lord.'

Wonderful it always seemed to me that there could exist a prayer made specially for Mamie and Mildred and me; and even more wonderful that it should have in it words of such peculiar beauty. Sometimes a little suspicion fluttered into my mind that we were really meant to pray for Nuns and Sisters of Mercy, but I would not listen to this. I wanted the prayer for ourselves.

Not for years did I learn that the first two words in that Collect were really '*Assist us*'. How empty and desolate it then sounded in my ears, denuded of that sudden splendid cry to heaven for '*The sisters*', left henceforth to wander bewildered, undefended among the changes and chances of this mortal life! Still, to have heard it thus wrong for the first ten years of my life gives me, to this day, a sense of personal possession in that prayer. Those childish mistakes were among the things which made the practice of family prayers most worth while.

People sometimes enjoy discussing what it is which makes the most fundamental difference between life to-day, and life in Queen Victoria's time. I should say it was something like this. Nowadays, home life is almost entirely free from regulation of any kind. This does not mean that most people are individually more free than they were: it is a difference in orientation. The 'Leisured Classes' have almost ceased to exist, and nearly everybody has a profession or a 'Career'. Girls willingly exchange the conformities of family life for the independence of working all the week in a shop or an office. The young men who used to make up those Monday to Friday shooting parties are now in the city. Home life for all of these must be crowded into a breathless week-end. And even the slow rhythm of life in the country has become a perpetual syncopation. The accent is shifted. The beat no longer falls with the steady Common Time of organized domesticity. It is broken by motor cars and aeroplanes. Family life has adapted itself to embrace the unorganized jostle of the pavement, and few houses have an atmosphere of their own. This is a loss, but those who regret it must realize that it was only achieved because people were then ready to accept routine in their homes, and to realize that that routine was creating something which was worth creating.

I look back on my youth, and I see a regulated existence which is now almost inconceivable even for those of us for whom it was once the only imaginable mode of life. Social life was then so organized that it seemed to have a momentum of its own, independent of the idiosyncrasies, the wishes, or the convenience of individuals. It had been arranged to exhibit an acknowledged purpose in life, and a faith in what lay outside. This gave it dignity and character. More, it made it into

[73]

an artistic whole, though those who had planned it would
have been the last to look at it in that way. But having
been planned, it did not admit of alteration. The wheel
of our lives then rotated slowly. It was more powerful
than ourselves. Its spokes were the successive events of
the days, the weeks, the years. To those spokes we
were bound. We rotated with them. They moved and
happened independently of the whims of any individual. Family prayers was one of the spokes.

V

Old Viney shared with our gardener what they call in North Wilts a Splittus, or house split between two families. It had originally been one of the small cloth-mills or factories which were common in Wilton in the eighteenth century, and the mill stream dived underground to pass beneath it. In the middle was a large brick hall, its roof supported by a wooden pillar, and the two households lived on either side of this. Viney always wore a white smock frock, which was most becoming to his tall figure. He had been the driver of the last mail coach which went over the hill to the Chalke Valley, and he used to tell us that before starting down the steep and narrow hill which goes from the Race Plain to Coombe Bissett, he always pulled up his horses and listened. If he heard no sound of creaking wheels or lumbering cart, he said to the guard: 'Start blowing.' The guard blew his horn, and he went on blowing while Viney whipped up his horses and galloped them headlong from top to bottom of the hill. The road lies between high banks, where there is no room to pass. Once they were off, nothing could have pulled up the

[75]

horses, and if anyone had begun to come up the hill
when the coach's mad career had begun, it must have
been the end of them all.

Viney was a boy at the time of Queen Victoria's
Coronation, and he made up his mind to go to London
to see the sight. He and a boy friend set off to walk
from Wilton. Before they reached Andover, the companion fell out, with blistered feet, and Viney walked
on alone. About twenty miles from London, he was
overtaken by an empty hearse, returning from a funeral
in the country. The driver offered him a lift, and in this
lugubrious vehicle Viney made his entrance into London. When the Coronation day came, he walked to the
door of the Abbey, no man saying him Nay, and there
he stood to watch the Queen get out of her carriage.
As he said, he 'could have touched her'. So easy
were things in those days for anyone who saw no preliminary difficulty in first walking eighty-four miles,
on the chance of seeing the Queen, and then, making
no further fuss about it, walking eighty-four miles
home again.

To-day, walking is no longer a recognized means of
getting from one place to another. It is only a recreation. As such, it has its own delight, yet a dignity has
departed from it since it ceased to be an accepted mode
of transit. In the twelfth century, Brother Samson
walked to Rome and back with a message to the Pope
from his monastery in England; and when he returned
to learn that his king, Richard Cœur de Lion, was a
prisoner somewhere in Hungary, he at once walked
off to look for him there. Even in my own day, Hilaire

Belloc walked to Rome, and made about that journey the most delightful of his books.

Viney was not the only man of his day to walk to London from Wiltshire. A few years earlier, there had been Mr. Brown, who constituted himself the voluntary caretaker of Stonehenge. He loved the stones, and watched them summer and winter, always ready to talk of them to the rare visitors who appeared; and during his many hours alone there, he was at work on his own masterpiece. This was a plaster model to scale of Stonehenge as he saw it in the first quarter of the nineteenth century. Every stone was modelled with the utmost care, and while the work was in process, nothing interrupted the artist, except an occasional walk to Salisbury, nine miles away, to buy fresh materials. When it was finished, Mr. Brown offered it to the British Museum, and it was accepted. He put no trust in the professional carriers of his day. He resolved to take it to London himself. So he put his beloved work of art on to a pair of trucks, and wheeled it direct from Salisbury Plain to the museum. The most surprising thing about that journey is that it only took two days and two nights. He pushed his barrow into the courtyard, and showed the porter his letter from the trustees, which he had carried up in his pocket. Without further question, the two men then carried the model into the hall and set it down there. Then, Mr. Brown turned on his heel, took up the handles of his truck, and wheeled it empty back to Stonehenge.

He was indeed a walker of the old type. Wherever he wished to go, he went on foot, walking as easily and

[77]

naturally about the Plain as a plover lollops over it on the wing. He was one of the native archæologists of Wiltshire, and he often gave lectures to learned societies in Salisbury. On those mornings, he was up early, so as to be sure that all his drawings, maps, and charts should be in the lecture-room by night. They were too many to be carried all at once. He carried the first instalment to Salisbury in the morning, and then walked back to dine at Amesbury, having completed his first eighteen miles. After dinner, he walked off again with the rest of his papers, lectured in the evening and walked home at night.

Mr. Brown was eventually taken ill and died at Winchester in 1839, in the course of a walk to give one of his lectures at Chichester.

He was before my day; but I well remember Mr. Inman, the Rector of West Knoyle, who fixed a telescope outside his house, so that through it he could scan the immense road which connects his village with the outer world. Through this telescope, he could recognize, many miles away, the walking figure of any of his clerical friends. The clergyman could be seen while he was still three or four hours away, yet, in that lonely neighbourhood, West Knoyle Rectory was undoubtedly the only possible destination of the inevitably approaching dot. Then Mr. Inman ran to the poultry yard to kill a chicken which was roasted and ready for dinner by the time the hungry pedestrian arrived.

What a lonely, lovely mode of life is recalled by this picture! The quiet empty downland. The solitary figure moving steadily towards its goal. Mr. Inman's dramatic gesture of pleasure and surprise as he met his friend at the door. Then the delicious home-made meal; the two voices talking late into the night while Mrs. Inman tossed on her feather-bed overhead; the well-earned sleep, undisturbed by the hoarse voices of the sheep or their tinkling bells, the sounds of which floated continuously through the window all through the night; then, next morning, once more, the long road.

Those walkers knew every yard of their country roads, while the motorist of to-day can barely catch sight of the milestones which flash past him as he roars relentlessly by.

When they first married, my parents often walked out to dinner with their friends in the neighbouring villages. This meant a walk of three miles over the hill to dine with Archdeacon Lear at Bishopstone: it was three miles up the Wylye valley to find Archdeacon Buchanan at Wishford: while the Penruddockes at Compton Chamberlayne were six miles away. People dined early then, and it must have been very pleasant to stroll through the late summer afternoon for dinner at half-past six or seven, and afterwards to return in the deep twilight. In dry weather, the roads shewed white in the night, and little traffic came to stir up the dust, when once the farm horses had been brought home after their day's work.

The downs all round were utterly still, though now and again a train roared by, followed by a sulky red glare of smoke which lit for a few moments the darkening sky.

By my day, my parents did not walk to dinner farther than to Wilton House, a quarter of a mile from the Rectory. In fine weather we never drove there, but pinned our long frilled voluminous skirts round our waists, and wore goloshes over our satin shoes. One of mine came off one evening, in a dark slough of slippery mud, and I never knew it till I reached Wilton House, while my sister Mamie once forgot all about hers and went in to dinner with them still on her feet. But the long skirts of those days hid a multitude of sins.

A short time before the war, I saw a man who was taking a most romantic walk. My father and I were driving from Wilton to Wilsford, and on Camp Hill we overtook a flock of sheep which had spread themselves over the grass on either side of the zigzag road. My father was at once interested, as he did not recognize the breed. Later in the day, when we were coming home, we met them again, and then my father got out of the carriage to have a talk with the shepherd. He was a Dorset man, employed by a farmer in that county, who owned what was indeed one of the only two flocks in England of this particular breed. Every year part of the flock was exchanged with the other, which belonged to a Hertfordshire farmer. The sheep were frightened and upset if they travelled by train, and even in pre-war days there was too much traffic on the main roads to make the journey from farm to farm a pleasant one. So this shepherd had for years driven his sheep by lanes and by-ways from county to county in the month of May. Their pace averaged two miles an hour, and the journey each way took three weeks. All along the route, the man now knew fields into which he could turn his sheep for the night, houses where he himself could find a bed, or inns which would give accommodation both to himself and his flock. When he reached Hertfordshire, he rested there for a week or two, and then drove back to Dorset the sheep he had come to fetch. There could not be a more ideal way of spending the months of May and June. I wonder if this Arcadian pilgrimage still continues, but I fear not, as there can hardly still be in the south of England enough forgotten tracks to allow a shepherd and his sheep to saunter through them from Dorset to Hertfordshire at a pace of two miles an hour.

My father loved walking. Every day he walked about his parish, and in and out of the houses of his parishioners. He was so completely at home in these, that he often opened the doors and went in without knocking, though this once gave him rather an awkward experience. He walked one day into a kitchen, in which the lady of the house was having her Saturday afternoon's bath. She heard his quick determined step as he approached, and jumping out of her tub, she crouched behind some linen which was airing on a horse before the fire. My father saw her at once, but with complete sang-froid, he quickly crossed the kitchen, and, looking up the stairs, he called the lady's name. When he got no answer, he turned on his heel and went quickly away, muttering to himself his disappointment at finding her not at home.

At one time we went through a phase of writing

each other's epitaphs, and one of my brothers wrote
this about my father:

> *Here lies the body of the Reverend Dacres,*
> *The friend of grocers and butchers and bakers.*
> *He walked so fast*
> *That at the last*
> *He walked right into the undertaker's.*

My father always walked in the country roads wearing a tall hat. His 'wide-awake' was only worn in the
garden. He thought it looked lazy, in spite of its name.
When he was over seventy, he had a bad carriage accident, and was thrown out of the carriage on to his
head. His tall hat saved his life, but curiously enough,
he took a dislike to it afterwards, and thenceforth he
only wore it in London.

I wonder what the people of to-day would say, if
they found themselves on one of the country roads of
my youth. Very muddy in winter, and very dusty in
summer, all their users had a share in making them.
In the autumn, cartloads of large flints were tipped into
piles by the roadside, and upon these the stone-breakers
set to work, wearing wire masks to protect their eyes
as they hammered the stones into pieces, which were
decreed to be 'no bigger than would go into a man's
mouth'. This measure was a very elastic one, to judge
by the size of the stones which were eventually spread
upon the roads. They were then slowly driven in by
the successive vehicles which passed over them in the
course of many months. As we drove about the country in the winter, we saw with despair ahead of us long

stretches of road covered with huge rough stones over which we had to pass. Those weary drags over the newly laid stones were our chief experiences in the course of our winter drives. The unhappy horses crept along, heads down, and feet painfully picking a way through the sharp, loose stones, while considerate drivers got out of their carriages and walked beside them. Everyone carried tools with which to pick out the stones which often lodged in the horseshoes, and too often lamed the horses.

Naturally everyone tried to follow in a track which had already begun to be levelled by someone in front, so one half of the road became more or less mended while the other half was practically untouched. Then the authorities devised the diabolical plan of laying down hurdles upon the levelled half, and so forcing the unhappy road users to begin their task once more upon the other side. Mr. Savage once leapt out of his carriage and triumphantly threw the hurdles over the hedge into the field. This was an offence against the road acts, and he was prosecuted and severely fined.

Then the first steam-rollers appeared, and these added a fresh terror to the roads, as very few horses would pass them at work. There were exciting scenes when horses shied, reared, leapt over hedges, turned sharp round, or bolted in the opposite direction while their drivers tried to coax them past these road monsters. Frightened ladies waved their whips at the red-flagged man who gave warning that a 'mechanically propelled vehicle' was approaching; and at this signal, he was bound by law to stop his engine and to lead the frightened animal by. This of course delayed matters, so many roads were never steam-rolled at all, but were left to be levelled in the old way by the casual passer-by.

VI

* ENTERTAINMENTS *

When I was a girl, country places were far more self-supporting in the way of entertainments than they are to-day. Nowadays, the smallest villages are generally within reach of a cinema; and for those who want to hear music of any kind, there is always the wireless. But in those days, when we wanted amusement, we had to produce it ourselves and our entertainments were often very good ones. At Wilton in my childhood we had a brass band which possessed some very loud and discordant instruments: its repertoire was small and its members never learnt quite perfectly any of the tunes they played, but it looked very important when it marched out on ceremonial occasions. We also had a fife and drum band for merriment, a Choral Society which studied serious music, a troop of Christy Minstrels, and my eldest sister's 'Girls' Class', which could always sing a cantata. Then there was Fred Rawlence, who in winter arranged tableaux vivants in the Talbot and Wyvern Hall, and in summer he sometimes had a wonderful torchlight pageant in his garden at Bulbridge at night. Edward Slow, our Wiltshire poet, was delighted to step upon the stage and to read extracts from his dialect poems; and at the Rectory we could always produce a good dramatic company.

The Christy Minstrel Troupe had two excellent corner men, Frank Brazier and Ernest Ridout. They were a most spirited pair and were full of quips and riddles. One series of riddles, which never failed to bring the house down, was based on Christian names. They asked each other: 'Have you seen Ann?' 'Ann who?' 'Anemone,' and so on for at least ten minutes at a time. Once the questioner got confused and said: 'Have you seen Tommy?' The other corner man was puzzled by this and he shook his head gravely, saying: 'No, I ain't seen Tommy.' There was another pause, and then came: 'Then have you seen Tom?' Great relief. 'Tom who?' '*Tomato.*'

Of course such little slips appealed very much to the audience.

In its palmiest days, the Christy Minstrel Troupe numbered about thirty men, and one evening we added to their number by setting in the midst of their row of black faces, a patch of ten or twelve women, elaborately made up and wearing white dresses and wigs. We then called them 'The Black and White Negro Troupe', and we made a very grand entrance, when my brother Reginald swung open the stage door and led us in, to the tune of 'Uncle Thomas walks like that'. As our large company stamped round and round the stage to this tune, a stranger in the audience was heard to ask Lady Pembroke: 'Who are these people?' The answer she received was: 'It's the Miss

[86]

Oliviers and their brothers.' There were forty-two of us.

The great entertainment of the year was always held on the Tuesday in Easter week. It was a very old-fashioned function and I think my father must have brought the idea from Great Yarmouth, where he had been a curate in the late 'fifties. It was called the Church Helpers' Tea, and was attended by Church workers of every kind—school teachers, choirmen, bellringers, district visitors, holders of missionary boxes and what not. The hostesses were six of the chief ladies in the parish and they each presided at a long table which they had loaded with the most delicious food. As we each laid our tables, we eyed the others with envious glances, for there was immense rivalry between the hostesses. Nowadays such a party would be considered very banal, but people enjoyed it very much then. After tea, the plates and dishes were cleared away and replaced by cards, draughts, dominoes and letter games. For the next two hours, the guests happily played away at these games, exchanged the latest gossip, and listened to an occasional song by one of the local vocalists—'The Death of Nelson', and 'The Children's Home', were special favourites. At the end of the evening my father made a speech. He reported on the Church work of the year and he also said how many people had died in its course, and what their ages had been. Then he told us about the weather and gave a great many other statistics which he always succeeded in making supremely exciting. This speech, which sounds from its subject matter as if it must have been very commonplace, was always the climax of the evening. At its end we broke into a hymn:

> *'Through the night of doubt and sorrow*
> *Onward goes the Pilgrim Band.'*

Then we separated for another year.

We once had a very picturesque entertainment which began with some children's tableaux, arranged by Fred Rawlence and ended with a Fairy Cantata sung by my sister's class of factory girls. They were charmingly dressed in white gowns, and wore stars on their heads with floating veils. Each carried a silver wand. We thought of a very ambitious and poetic opening to our cantata, singing the first chorus *pianissimo* before the curtain went up. The words were:

> *Would'st thou know what sounds are stealing*
> *Through these fair and rural bowers?*

As the exquisite notes stole into the room, we singers behind the scenes were aghast to hear the whole audience break into roars of laughter. We bravely sang on, unable to imagine what could have made our music appear farcical. It was not until the entertainment was over that we learnt that the stage, which had been raised about a foot for the children's tableaux, had been lowered for the cantata, while the curtain was left at its original height. There was therefore a considerable hiatus between it and the new stage level. The fairylike costumes of the chorus had not included their footwear, and, as they listened to the sentimental strains, the audience saw before their eyes about sixty somewhat clumsy ankles clothed in shapeless boots of all ages, most of them sadly trodden down at the heel. The effect was less fairylike than we had hoped.

Many of our entertainments were in aid of the Parish Nurse Fund, and at one of these, the Mayor, a crusted old Wiltshire character, made a speech which ended with this peroration.

'They say that all nurses are angels, but I'm sure I can truly say that *our* nurse is an exception to the rule.'

Nurse Turner was slightly deaf, and she smiled on serenely, quite unconscious of this somewhat left-handed compliment.

Perhaps the most amusing entertainment we ever had in Wilton was when we heard the Phonograph for the first time. This was a forerunner of the gramophone. You spoke or sang into it, and the record was immediately reproduced. The entertainer began by telling us that on his arrival in the town that evening, he had been fortunate enough to find the Wilton brass band practising in the hall, and that he had persuaded them to allow him to make a record on the spot. He then proceeded to let us hear this record. Until then, most of the audience had imagined that the phonograph was only an elaborate trick, and that it could not truly reproduce actual sounds heard at the time. Now in one minute we realized that it could indeed do all that its producer boasted. Out there streamed into the room the favourite tune of the Wilton band, well known to everybody present, played by those instruments whose harsh discordant timbre had for years led our club processions to church. Every familiar mistake was reproduced with cruel exactness. No entertainment could possibly have had a better or more appropriate overture.

The Mayor was now asked to make a speech into the phonograph. He was a nervous man and he was much embarrassed as he climbed on to the platform and, in sight of everyone, was confronted with the mouthpiece of this most tell-tale instrument. It made him more nervous than ever, and between each word he spoke, there came an agonized—'Er . . . er . . . er.' The audience listened entranced, knowing that this was about to be reproduced for their entertainment. In a few moments the poor Mayor's speech was repeated in a thin Punch-and-Judy voice, with little squeaks to represent those stutterings. The audience feared to lose the faintest of these absurd little sounds, so everybody stuffed their handkerchiefs into their mouths until the speech was over, and then came an outburst of laughter.

Undeterred by the Mayor's embarrassing experience, a town councillor then leapt on to the platform, certain that he would be able to make a success. He really was even more absurd. His enunciation was always rather ridiculous and precise, but he was delighted at the thought of his well-turned phrases being now perpetuated.

'When in *Chicahgo* in April *lahst*,' he began, 'I had the great pleasure of listening to Mr. Edison's voice on the phonograph. It gives me great pleasure *heah* to congratulate him on his invention and to thank him for the pleasant hours we are enjoying this evening.'

The self-satisfaction in the speaker's tone came back when the speech was reproduced with a very funny effect.

There is more to be said of this precisely speaking man. He was then Managing Director of the Wilton Carpet Factory, a very pious person and a strong tee-totaller. The visit to Chicago of which he spoke that night was one of many, for he often went to the States, and he founded there a branch of the Wilton Carpet Factory. He died very suddenly, and his death was a great shock to the town, for no one had even heard that he was ill. He now was laid in state upon his bed, while the factory employés filed through the room in long lines, to see his face for the last time. As she went by, one of the factory girls was bold enough to lay her finger upon the dead man's cheek, and then she sprang back, exclaiming:

'Ain't he warm!'

After this no further visitors were admitted to the room.

Two days later, as was the case with Tennyson's Enoch Arden, it might have been said of Wilton that the little town—

'Had seldom seen a costlier funeral.'

The procession was two miles long and the orations delivered over the grave by ministers of various denominations were if anything even longer.

Then followed an unexpected sequel. In transpired that this seemingly righteous man had been living a double life. He was no teetotaller in London or in the States, but had there spent his evenings entertaining chorus girls, and in drinking in restaurants. He had made away with a large amount of money belonging to the company which owned the factory. Its shareholders were ruined, and half the population of Wilton was out of work till a new company could be formed. The world marvelled at the fortunate appropriateness of his death; but those who lived near by reported that, on the night after the funeral, a mysterious, veiled widow, in height and proportions curiously resembling the dead man, had been seen to leave his house, and to drive away in a cab to an unknown destination.

The lettering on the grave in the cemetery has long ago faded out.

VII

★ THE OLDEST INHABITANT ★

These words fill one with a passionate curiosity and hope, nearly always to be disappointed. The oldest inhabitant often has no desire to speak of his memories, and when he does speak, the things he remembers are seldom those which his questioner hopes to hear. When Mr. W. H. Hudson was walking about Wiltshire collecting materials for his book *A Shepherd's Life*, he asked my father to direct him to some of the old people who might be likely to tell him things. They did not guess that he was a writer, for he looked, as he was, a very unassuming wayfaring fisherman, but in spite of that, he could not make them speak. Day after day he drew a blank.

The old Wilton people were generally ready to talk to my father, because they knew him so well, but their memories often meant nothing at all to anyone except themselves. He once asked old Francis, who was nearly a hundred, what was the first thing he could remember.

He remained quite silent for some minutes, sinking back into the past. Then, very slowly, he said:

'I can mind when dthurteen vlocks did come to water to Bull Bridge.'

Like many of the most outstanding memories of
country people, this was a memory of a year of exceptional weather. There had been a drought. But old
Francis could not remember when it was. Only 'a
long time ago'.

My sister Mildred once gave a Nonagenarian tea-
party, her guests being three very vigorous old women.
Mrs. Blake was the wife of a smallholder, and in my
childhood she was often to be seen driving three cows
through the street. She was extremely practical, and
refused to trouble about the past. The present was still
her concern; and when we sat in the garden after tea,
trying to make the old women talk, she pretended no
interest in our conversation. With her face twisted to
one side, her shrewd observant eyes were watching
the gardener drive the ducks to bed. The silly birds
were quite out of hand, straying off in all directions.
Mrs. Blake could not tolerate this independence. She
jumped from her seat, and running like a girl, she
headed off one after the other the birds which had wandered the farthest, and got them back into line. Then
she joined the gardener, and walked proudly behind the
flock to the yard.

Meanwhile, Mildred asked Mrs. Jeffery if she could
tell us her real age.

'I were barn', she said, 'in the year afore were all that
there hanging and killing.'

She was exasperated when my sister could not
recognise this date.

'*You know*,' she said. 'It's in the Spelling Book.'

We hopefully thought of the French Revolution.

But no, that would make Mrs. Jeffery at least a hundred and twenty. We guessed again and again, showing ourselves in the old woman's eyes as complete half-wits, and at last found that 'hanging and killing' was Mrs. Jeffery's impression of the Battle of Waterloo.

Granny Hayden of Netherhampton to the day of her death was a delightful companion. She was nearer a hundred than ninety when she stood merrily at her wash tub in the yard behind her cottage, declaring that the secret of her perpetual youth was that she 'Never ran up Harnham Hill to meet trouble,' a real proverb in the making. She possessed a splendid old crinoline dress which she had worn as a young woman, and she also had lots of bright coloured shawls. On St. George's day, she was always ready to dress up in some of her old clothes and 'step out' in the village procession, laughing and enjoying it with all her might.

At the Mothers' Meeting one afternoon, Mrs. Hayden was suddenly inspired to relate some of her early memories.

'I can mind', she began, 'when Mr. Tom Wiles used to turn the barrel organ in church. 'Twer down be'ind the font, and the font 'e wurden the same one as it is now. 'E wur made o' white stone, and all the church wer different then. 'Twas afore the restoration, see. I can mind when we 'ad a barrel organ in the barn for the first Jubilee. 'Twas for the dancing, and Mr. Taunton 'e led off wi' Mrs. Terrell, and when 'e couldn't get anyone to stand up wi' un, he danced wi' a dog. Took un 'old by his front paws 'e did. I can mind the last one as was transported for stealing sheep. He was from

Quidhampton, and 'e took un up to Bedford's Folly and killed un there, and then the police come in, and they found the 'ead and the trotters in the room. My 'usband went to see someone 'anged at Salisbury. He stood up and spoke to the people, and then the bolt come down. My 'usband said as he never wanted to see another.'

Mrs. Hayden's mention of sheep-stealing, recalls a letter written long ago by Mr. Squarey of Downton, to Lady Jeane Petherick, then a child in her home at Longford.

'My brother-in-law, Edward Hodding, was the tenant of Odstock Farm about the year 1837–38, and one late frosty evening in the winter, he and his shepherd Thomas Selfe, having taken a last look at their sheep which were folded near the Little Yews, were walking home. As they neared the road which leads by Odstock Wood to Odstock, Mr. Hodding looked round (I dare say he was scant of breath after walking up the hill), and saw a faint column of smoke rising out of the Great Yews. They speculated what it could mean, and then concluded they would try to find out. So back they trudged by Catherine's Barn, and on and on till they could nearly fix the spot where the smoke still rose before them. They crept quietly onwards through the yew trees, and at last, in a pit, they espied three men sitting round a fire, over which was hanging, from two forked sticks, a leg of mutton being roasted. Hodding and his shepherd were plucky men, and they rushed on them, each catching hold of one man. The other bolted off, not staying to finish his roast mutton!

'With their prisoners, they walked down to Odstock, and thence to Salisbury jail (there were no police then), where they were taken in charge.

'Their companion was not caught. The two were brought to trial, when it was proved by the marks on the sheep's skin found near, that it had been stolen from a flock near Martin. Enquiry after they were taken, led to the discovery that many sheep had been stolen from distant flocks, and brought to the home of these gentry at the Great Yews to be eaten or sold when opportunity offered.

'The thieves were convicted and sentenced to transportation. The farmers around counted their flocks more regularly thereafter, but sheep-stealing ceased to be a regular profession after the breaking up of this gang.

'Now I will tell the pathetic story of Joshua Scamp, who lies buried in Odstock churchyard. It is well that you should know that your great great grandfather, Lord Radnor, and my father, knew all the circumstances that I am about to relate, and did their utmost to procure a mitigation of the sentence which had been passed on him for horse-stealing.

'Odstock was a great gathering place at the time of the gipsies, who were then much more numerous than at present. They kept themselves more aloof and as a separate people. They had, and still have I believe their own language. I will not discuss the mysterious and interesting origin of these people, but merely say that they were then, as they still are in some degree, regarded more or less as outcasts and robbers.

'Late in 1800 or early in 1801, a horse had been stolen in the neighbourhood, and suspicion fell on Joshua Scamp, whose tent was near. He was taken up and tried at the Assizes at Salisbury, and was convicted and sentenced to death, which was the penalty for horse- and sheep-stealing, and formerly other petty crimes which are now (thank God) more leniently dealt with.

'After his conviction, he persisted in asserting his innocence, and implied that he knew who the culprit was, but refused to disclose his name.

' "No," he said, "I am an old man, and it is better for me to hang than the real man."

'My father from whom I heard this story, and who had then only just come to Salisbury, and many others, were convinced that Scamp was telling the truth, and they interested your ancestor in their efforts to procure a reprieve. But there were no telegraphs or quick posts in those days, and the short interval between conviction and execution ebbed fast away, before the Home Office authorities could be impressed with the circumstances. So, at the appointed time, Joshua Scamp walked bravely to the gallows asserting his innocence, but silent as to who was really guilty.

'After his death, it became known that the real thief was Joshua Scamp's son-in-law, who had married his favourite daughter, for love of whom the old man was content to bear the penalty which should have fallen on her husband.

'The gipsies placed a tomb over his grave in Odstock churchyard, which still stands, and for many years they were in the habit of visiting his resting-place in large numbers on the anniversary of his death, April 1st, 1801.

'And now please Lady Jeane, do you and your brothers and sisters make a pilgrimage to the grave of Joshua Scamp, and think of the unselfish love and self-sacrifice for his daughter's sake, of the convicted, but innocent, horse-stealer, Joshua Scamp.'

A contemporary of Mr. Squarey's was Canon Jackson, who used to tell us another exciting old Wiltshire story. I am not sure whether or not he was actually present, but he well remembered that dark night in October 1816, when, as the London coach stopped at Winterslow Hut to deliver the mails, there broke upon the surrounding silence a terrifying roar, and a lioness leapt out from the dark ominous spaces of Salisbury Plain. Canon Jackson gave a graphic account of the battle between the lioness and one of the coach horses, which fought furiously with its forefeet, striking at its enemy with its iron hoofs. He had nearly got her down, when he became entangled in the harness, and the lioness sprang upon his chest and hung there, her claws fastened into his throat, while blood spurted in all directions. Then there appeared upon the scene an enormous dog, which made a rear attack upon the lioness. She let go the horse, and turned upon this new enemy. The dog alternately attacked and withdrew, drawing the lioness after him towards what Canon Jackson used to call a 'hovel', which seems to have been a shed with a door which could be fastened. Here followed the last terrific fight, ending for the moment in victory for the lioness. The dog was killed. But reinforcements were now prepared. All this time, the innkeeper, the coach officials and the passengers had merely watched the amazing fight. They felt fairly safe so long as the animals were frantically engaged. Now the tremendous noise had called up the owners of the circus from which the lioness had escaped. Their vans were a short way up the road. By now they were on the spot. The mysterious 'mastiff' had, in the last round of his fight, lured the lioness inside the shed, and the spectators had the courage to shut the door. The cage was then brought up against it, and the lioness was successfully captured.

This blood-curdling scene took place while Hazlitt was living in Winterslow, and it did not change his opinion of the peacefulness of the place. His *Winterslow Essays* suggest that one is not likely to meet there any animal fiercer than a bookworm, although as a matter of fact it has always been something of a magnet for lions. Hazlett himself of course, and then his admirer, Lord Grey of Falloden, in later days sometimes tried vainly to inspire distinguished American visitors with his own enthusiasm for the plain little inn with its sober associations with the prose of the countryside. I heard one such guest openly avow her preference for 'a *cassle*'.

Yet another lion to find himself in a dilemma at Winterslow was Siegfried Sassoon who once found his car and himself in a pond at the door of the inn, as he was driving from London in a thick fog. The owners retaliated by putting up a notice saying—

THIS POND IS PRIVATE

Another Winterslow character was Lyddie Shears, the witch, whose son had often been seen in my day by the oldest inhabitants—an old man, wandering about the ruins of his mother's cottage. Lyddie herself lived I think quite early in the nineteenth century, and, like other witches, she had a way with hares. The poachers gave her presents of tobacco and snuff, and thus primed, she went on to the downs in the moonlight and, crouching low on the ground, she struck lights from flints. All about her, there then popped up startled heads with long quivering ears and mad eyes glancing from side to side. The poacher shot the hares while they sat thus, dazzled and bewildered.

Lyddie was not so friendly with a neighbouring farmer who was less generous with his tobacco than the poachers were. When he was going coursing, he never omitted to ask Lyddie to tell him where he would find a hare that morning, and her answers always proved right. Then, time and again, the greyhounds ran it to the same place, the field at the back of Lyddie's cottage, and there they always lost it. At last the disappointed farmer was advised by a friend, who knew something of the black arts, to make a bullet from a sixpence, and with that to shoot the hare just before it reached the crucial spot. He did so, but the hare vanished as usual. That evening a neighbour, calling upon Lyddie Shears, found her lying dead in her cottage, with a silver bullet through her heart.

The hare is the English werewolf, though she seems a frightened harmless creature to keep company with witches. Mrs. Morrison told me of a witch drama in

South Wales, with a strong family likeness to the story
of Lyddie Shears. This witch was a middle-aged woman living with her old mother, and she too was
credited with the power of changing herself into a
hare. All the troubles in the district were laid at her
door. She put spells on the ewes and they died in lambing: she dried up the cows: she sent children into such
paroxysms of terror that they became imbeciles for life.

Mrs. Morrison was one day walking near the witch's
cottage when she heard a gunshot. Almost immediately
she came upon one of her keepers, who said breath-
lessly:

'I've just shot Ruth Colt.'

'Shot her?' exclaimed Mrs. Morrison, aghast.

'Yes. I caught her coming out of the cowshed, and
when she saw me, she ran away. I went after her, and
just outside her own door, I saw her change into a hare.
I fired, and she fell, but she got up again, and she
managed to get indoors. But I think I've done for her.'

Mrs. Morrison walked about the fields, pondering
over this extraordinary story, and last she made up her
mind to call upon the Colt family. The old mother
came to the door, and invited her to come in. They sat
talking by the fire.

'Is Ruth out?' asked Mrs. Morrison at last.

'No. She's in bed. She's not well.'

Mrs. Morrison was then allowed to visit the invalid,
and found her lying in bed with a large patch of blood
on the front of her nightgown. An abscess was said to
have broken in her chest.

From the stories told by oldest inhabitants, it would

seem that until about 1860, the countryside was haunted by congregations of witches. Many people testify to having seen and known them, but the witnesses, like the witches, are dead. It is a curious phase of human history, and the attitude of their neighbours towards them was also curious. It was a mixture of toleration, fear, and respect, changing into actual antagonism only after the witch had gone to the length of becoming a hare. But I know one Wiltshire witch story of a later date, and it is vouched for by a panel doctor, which gives it a very matter-of-fact local-government atmosphere.

Within the last twenty years, there lived in a village near Wilton a man who was such a complete neurasthenic that he had not even the energy to walk down the street to the surgery, but, day in and day out, he sat by his own fireside, bent and bowed in sullen gloom. He had hardly the wits to answer the doctor's questions when his club certificate had to be signed. After some years of this semi-imbecility, the man one morning walked briskly into the surgery, and asked to be signed off. He returned at once to work, and he remained at it.

A week or two later, the doctor heard the story which was believed by all the village. When the man had been ill for five years, a friendly neighbour offered to consult a witch who lived a few miles away. The witch pronounced that the man had had the evil eye 'put on him' by two Warlocks, but she could not utter the names of these monsters, as this would 'add to their power'. She produced photographs of them, and she

promised to 'break the spell'. This she did in a manner
which was never explained, but which was so effective
that within a few weeks, both the sorcerers 'died rav-
ing—a judgment of God for the wickedness they had
done'. The witch would take no fee, and on the morning after the second of his two enemies had been buried,
the bewitched man had come to see the doctor.

My father's two old sisters were wonderful racon-
teuses, and if they would, they could have told us some
good stories of Wiltshire in the old days. Unluckily
they entered with such violent prejudice into all the
contemporary family events, that when they had finished with the misdemeanours of their nephews and
nieces they had few words left for the past. But Aunt
Margaret Bruce could sometimes be drawn, and then
she was always entertaining.

She was staying once in a house where Keble was a
fellow guest, and one evening their host read aloud,
with great enthusiasm, *The Raven* of Edgar Allen Poe.
In the impressed silence which followed, Mr. Keble
remarked:

'Don't you think it would have been better if that
had never been printed?'

Thomas Moore was in those days a neighbour, and
he often came to Potterne to hear my grandmother
sing his 'Irish Melodies'. She had a very beautiful
voice, and he used to stand by the piano as she sang,
regulating her interpretation by gestures with his hands.
He also liked to be asked to sing his own songs, and he
sang one night at Wans when Aunt Margaret was
there. During the song, two of the guests exchanged

a whispered remark. Tommy Moore was extremely conceited and touchy, and now he seized his music and rushed out of the room. In the awed silence which followed, the front door slammed loudly. Unfortunately the poet possessed no bump of locality, and though Wans was very near to his cottage at Sloperton, he lost his way and wandered all night. His wife thought he was dead, but the next morning he was seen in a neighbouring field, sitting quietly on a gate waiting for someone to pass by and tell him where he was.

A good deal might be written about the things which the oldest inhabitant has forgotten to tell. There was, for instance, the Lord Radnor who died without telling his successor the whereabouts of some papers essential to the ownership of Longford. The wife of the heir was that intrepid spiritualist of whom I have already spoken, and although in his lifetime her father-in-law's temper had been such that no one ever dared ask him an awkward question, yet now she dauntlessly called him back from the shades. There was no doubt as to the identity of the ghost who returned. Lord Radnor's vigorous language was easily recognizable; and now in his well-known idiom, he told the family what they wanted to know, and the lost papers were discovered.

The beautiful Elizabeth Countess of Pembroke must have been, when she died in 1831, Wilton's oldest inhabitant. Two years before this, she had carried into Hoare's Bank in Fleet Street, a locked box to be deposited in one of the strong rooms. There it remained when she died, for she had told none of her family about it; and there it lay unclaimed for eighty years. Its existence was quite unknown to the then Lord Pembroke when Messrs. Hoare asked him his wishes about it. The box was sent to Wilton, but no key could be found for it. It was forced open, and then there was disclosed a treasure which sounds more like the *Arabian Nights* than a Wiltshire country house at the beginning of the twentieth century. Displayed on a series of trays was the celebrated collection of gems made by Cardinal Mazarin, and which had been the talk of Europe three hundred years before.

Lady Pembroke knew what she was doing when she handed those jewels to Messrs. Hoare, and then died without saying anything about them. Her son George Augustus had died in 1827, and his successor Robert (the 'wicked' though charming and romantic earl) was living in Paris, where he made a practice of selling any heirloom on which he could lay his hands. Lady Pembroke had not the power to will the Mazarin gems away from the head of the family, but at ninety-two she still possessed the tact and judgment which had not failed her throughout her long and difficult life. Her loyalty and wisdom told her what to do. She kept silence, and she also kept the Mazarin jewels for the Pembroke family.

VIII

★ CLOCKS AND CALENDARS ★

When St. Augustine was asked what he thought on the nature of time, he replied: 'When I think of it, I know. When I speak of it, I cannot say,' and most people would agree with the second part of this pronouncement. Baron von Hügel habitually used two different words when he spoke of time, for he was both a profound thinker and a careful speaker, and he would use twenty words where other people would use one, if he could thus express more clearly and candidly what he had in mind. The Baron spoke of '*Time*' and of '*Clock-Time*', and this distinction is now used by many other writers. Countrymen will easily respond to its truth and delicacy. The nearer one lives to nature, the more one realizes the artificial character of that clock-time by which town-dwellers automatically and unquestioningly regulate their lives. To this day, when the true Wiltshireman wants to know the time, a clock is the last thing he will consult. He looks at the sun or the shadows, or at the smoke of a far-off passing train.

Yet we had timepieces in Wiltshire when the rest of

England had not even thought of wanting them. Mrs. Markham first taught me that King Alfred told the time by candles painted with coloured bands of regular widths, and these early clocks were of Wessex invention. But their use was never very general, and most people still watched the sun in the heavens, rather than the candle in the house.

The oldest clock in Wiltshire is centuries older than King Alfred and his candles. It is Stonehenge, which ignores the hours, and tells the time of the year rather than of the day. Stonehenge is indeed the holy place of an ancient religion, but it also told the men of that religion, as it tells the men of to-day, the dates of the summer and the winter solstices, as well as the equinoxes in autumn and in spring. It is almost a disaster that so many people have now heard that on the longest day, the sun rises over the Hele Stone far away to the east of the circle, throwing its long shadow upon the Altar Stone in the centre. This quiet miracle of the dawn was once an object of pilgrimage: now it is a centre of jollification. On the evening before the longest day, a hurly-burly of charabancs can be seen and heard converging upon Stonehenge. These disgorge a crowd of merry-makers who spend some jolly hours drinking barrels of beer and bottles of 'mineral water'—a dreary phrase which it is impossible to associate with the merry pop of ginger beer. Gramophones and other noises keep this rout awake till sunrise, but they would be far more sure of getting what they want, if they stayed in Bournemouth and went to a cinema, where a good sunrise can be guaranteed without exposure to rough weather, and without disturbing the shepherds of Salisbury Plain.

Those Plain-dwellers watch the sun all round the year, and he regulates their lives and their work. Clock-time is not for them, and their hours cannot be codified as if they worked in factories at the call of sirens and whistles. Their times and seasons are nature's own.

Many farmers dislike summer time, but it is at least an acknowledgement of the truth, that day and night are not the same thing in summer and in winter. To me, living in the country, summer time is pure joy. I can never forget the first day when that miraculous movement of the clock seemed suddenly to release upon us in one day all the sunshine of a summer. It was May 21st, 1916, and life had for many months been darkened for us by the war. I am convinced that the sun was confused by the change in the clocks, so that he shone that day for more hours than he knew. We were in London, and my brother Reginald suggested a drive into the country, so we drove away from our own troubled times and back into the eighteenth century, down the Avenue in Bushey Park where the chestnut trees were lit by their thousands of flowery chandeliers. Then to Hampton Court, where man has for long dominated nature, and where the art of one generation has never feared to impose itself upon the work of bygone predecessors.

The huge bell of the palace clock was indeed striking that day for the first time, an hour ahead of the sun, but at Hampton Court, the human race expects to be supreme. Wolsey's Tudor Palace had accepted the new formality of Wren's Fountain Court: horticulture had produced in the English climate those stupendous bunches of grapes which rivalled Joshua's spoils from Palestine: the formal eighteenth century flower beds had been adapted to the free grace of flowers grown to accord with the taste of another day. The royal palace knows how to adapt itself to the vagaries of kings, and Hampton Court obeyed the new law of Summer Time, with a zest unequalled elsewhere.

Nature too rejoiced in the sun. At luncheon in a copse near Chertsey we saw the clear liquid rays work miracles as they slipped through the pale green foliage of the birches, and at Ascot, the azaleas in my uncle's garden smelt like Hymettus honey. We reached Windsor in the evening. There we stayed, watching the long-delayed sunset lighting the castle walls when night had begun at last to creep over the forest trees in the park. It was unforgettable—the red flame which illuminated that vast conglomeration of buildings, where the passing centuries had slowly achieved a triumph of dignity and strength. Thus lit, in proud isolation, Windsor Castle seemed to be *plus royaliste que le roi.*

The coming each year of summer time always recalls to me that long lovely day, though putting on the clocks was no new thing at Wilton. Like the King at Sandringham, Sidney Lord Pembroke had always advanced his clocks half an hour in the shooting season, though this made endless confusions over fixing engagements with people who were keeping Greenwich time. The Wilton people called Lord Pembroke's manipulated clock-time 'The Lord's Day'.

On the downs, Lord's Day and Commoners' Day are lost in a wide awareness of the rise and fall of daylight which cannot be experienced by people who live in the valleys. The shepherds in their huts in the lambing season watch the eternal wonder of the sky, and so do the gipsies in their tents. I was nearest to it when I was once isolated by whooping-cough, and lived for three weeks in the grand stand on Salisbury Race Plain. There I saw the weather as never before, and I saw too, that if you can only see enough of it, all weather has beauty. My companion in exile was Foyle, our delightful maid, and we had great fun together, for she was an extremely racy conversationalist. We shared a bedroom, the only room in which it was possible to light a fire, and in it we lay, side by side, on camp beds.

On our first night, we had the worst thunderstorm of a generation, and half Wilton hurried up to see us next morning, convinced that the grand stand must have been struck by lightning. The storm made us feel very little and futile, as it roared round us, filling the sky with blazing darkness; and yet it was strangely exhilarating to be there alone on the downs, with all the powers of nature screaming past our room. We talked to one another in subdued voices during the din.

The storm was the opening of a fortnight of bad weather, and those wild days were wonderful to watch. I used to lie out in the shelter, watching the Cathedral as it changed its aspect every hour. Sometimes it appeared to be quite near by, and then it was of a brilliant transparent texture, lit up from within. A quarter of an hour later, it had receded into the distance, and stood miles away, a dull and sulky grey. Then it warmed to a deep yet threatening blue, after which it lost all appearance of solidity, and became an ethereal building of sunlit mist. In the evening it shone as red as the sunset which illuminated it; and often there played about it wide sheets or narrow spears of summer lightning, which shivered upon the delicately carved pinnacles of the spire.

Lots of people came to visit me in this beautiful isolation, riding up singly or in parties, driving pony-carts, or walking through the Hare Warren, for this was in 1907, when few country neighbours possessed motor cars. We often had large tea-parties, when the guests sat at the correct quarantine distance, and Foyle gave round tea and cakes. When everyone had gone home, we retired to our little sitting-room, with all round us the endless silence of the downs, and then, often, we heard again the thud of hoofs. Foyle hurried out to welcome the belated visitors, but no one could be seen, and the galloping horses passed invisibly by. We liked to think that we were hearing the echoes of the horse races of long ago, perhaps that one when even the bitterness of the Civil Wars did not prevent the bells of St. Thomas at Salisbury from ringing when Lord Pembroke won the Salisbury Cup.

These memories seem far from clocks and calendars, yet they lead back towards them. Years before my whooping-cough visit, my brother Frank had also been sent in quarantine to the Race Plain, where he lodged with the caretaker. These cottagers told the time by the smoke of the trains which passed in the valley. They got up by the milk train between four and five: they had breakfast by the paper train at half-past seven: the London express at half-past twelve was their dinner bell. If they had a clock, they did not use it or even wind it up.

More surprising than this, however, was the fact that many people living in the Square at Wilton, within sight of the town clock, preferred to tell the time by my father. He was the most punctual of men, and every morning in the week, he read Matins in the church at eight, and prayers at Wilton House at nine. He always walked through the Square at ten minutes to nine, and then the people set their watches, left to catch their trains, or started their day's work.

My brother Harold was for five years in a fort in Central Africa with a detachment of the King's African Rifles. In his district of twenty-thousand natives, no one possessed any means of measuring time. Harold was in fact their King Alfred, for he first taught them that it was possible to divide a day into hours. His watch became the town clock of the district, regulating the routine of his command. At last it went wrong, and then he made a sundial, and taught his soldiers to tell the time by it. Two buglers were always stationed beside it, bugling the hours as the shadow moved round. This gave immense delight to the people in the district, and all went well till the rainy season began. Then one morning two scared soldiers rushed in saying that 'the spirit was dead'. So indeed it was, till

the sun shone again. Afterwards Harold gave his
sergeants Waterbury watches, which made them very
proud.

These natives loved my brother, and when he came
home they wrote him many letters in their pictorial
language which contains few words for abstract ideas
like joy and sorrow.

'When we think of you, we laugh,' one of them
wrote. 'And when we think that you have gone away,
we cry.'

Those words said what we all felt after Harold had
been killed in France.

I hope that Easter will not become a fixed date as
long as I live, for when this is done, it will mean another long step taken towards the mechanization of
life. The changing date of Easter is in harmony with
our variable spring.

For people who live in towns, the calendars and time-
tables which can be bought in shops must be useful
and even indispensable, but primitive people, countrymen, and creative workers will continue to make their
own. What poet ever produced his poem on the date
scheduled by the publisher for its appearance? Probably other painters are like Rex Whistler, who never
buys an engagement book, but scribbles his dates on
to a long narrow strip of paper, always decorated with
absurd or graceful drawings. No one ever understood
better the convenience of his agricultural parishioners
than did Archdeacon Lear when he announced from
the pulpit that the next evening service would be on
the night of the full moon.

In his book *Farmer's Glory*, my friend and neighbour Mr. Street, writes of the farmers' year, as it unrolled itself before the eyes of a little boy between thirty and forty years ago. Ploughing in the autumn; lambing and sowing wheat after Christmas; putting in barley and oats in February and March; turnips in April; swedes and kale in May. Then followed the hay harvest, the corn harvest, and the root harvest. As he says: 'The system swept you with it, round and round, year after year, like a cog in a machine.' In truth, the system made the year. It *was* the year; and if ever Mr. Street found himself imprisoned for life in a sausage factory at Chicago, he would never get out of his bones, that sense of the pattern made for him by the months as they swung their unchanging round on Ditchampton Farm.

Half a mile away, we lived at the Rectory, in the orbit too of those agricultural seasons, and yet our year was not the farmer's year. We had our own. Ours was the Christian year.

Our year, like Mr. Street's, did not begin on January the first. Ann Thorp, my grandmother's old maid who lived with us, remarked each year on the 'dull, dark days before Christmas', and it was in these dull, dark days that our year began, with Advent Sunday. My father's preaching turn as a Prebendary of Salisbury often fell on the Sunday before Advent, and we generally went with him to the Cathedral Service that afternoon. So the approach of the new year was heralded for us by the anthem from Mendelssohn's 'Lobgesang'.

Watchman, will the night soon pass?
The night is departing, depar . . . ting. The day is approach-
ing, approa . . . ching.

The incredible high note was flung unto the arches in the pure fearless tones of the chorister. Each year I still hear in my mind those soaring notes of confidence in the 'dull, dark days before Christmas'.

Dull and dark they may have been, but they were busy days for us. We were counting the Sunday School marks, and buying the prizes, and then visiting old people to ask what they wanted as Christmas presents. They were always ready for our tap on the door, and had hardly opened it before their own answer rapped out: 'Trowsers', 'Blankets', or 'A dress length'. We noted this down and hastened back into the dull, dark weather. There were our own Christmas presents to make or buy, and we were often rehearsing a play to be performed directly after Christmas. And there were always the church decorations.

They were tremendous in those days. In the broad spaces between the windows were hung large red wooden shields upon which we emblazoned, in holly leaves and dyed everlasting flowers, mysterious eccle-siastical monograms and devices. This meant many pricked and hammered fingers. But the great under-taking each year was making the wreaths of evergreen, for over six hundred yards were required to twine round the pillars and to hang in festoons between them. The only place in Wilton which was big enough for this wreath-making was the Manège at Wilton House, with its sawdust-covered floor, and here we spent about ten days every December. Wooden benches were placed in rows down the length of the Manège, and upon these were laid pieces of rope, some of which were thirty and some forty-five feet long. One end of each piece was fastened to a nail at the end of the bench, and then we sat down and moved slowly backward, as we tied in the pieces of ilex, holly, box, and laurel, of which the festoon was composed. Our teacher was an old gardener, who had done this kind of thing all his life, and he was very strict about our technique. We had to sit 'straddle-legged', and to learn how to graduate the different lengths of stalk in our greenery, so as to make the festoon really strong. It was bitterly cold in the Manège, and round us, as we worked, there rose a cloud of thin dust, made of sawdust and pollen. It always gave me hay-fever, and I sneezed steadily all the time.

Thus described, those days before Christmas do indeed sound dull and dark, yet Advent had its heavenly splendour. Those heavy clouds were the right setting for the Advent hymn:

Lo He comes with clouds descending.

And as one thinks oneself back into those days, what emerges most distinctly is the memory of another austerely grand Gregorian tune:

Rejoice! Rejoice! Emmanuel
Shall come to thee O Israel.

The short winter days were illuminated by the terror, the majesty, and the joy of the Day of Doom.

For there were many extra services throughout
Advent and the hymn-tunes overflowed from the
church to the Manège, ringing in our heads as we
sneezed among the sawdust.

> *In Thy beauty all resplendent,*
> *In Thy glory all transcendent*
> *Well may we rejoice and sing.*
> *Coming! In the opening east*
> *Herald brightness slowly swells*
> *Coming! O my glorious Priest,*
> *Hear we not thy golden bells?*

I can never forget those radiant visions when Advent
comes back now. Every year I remember the old ardent
tunes:

> *Time appointed may be long*
> *But the vision must be sure.*
> *Certainty shall make us strong,*
> *Joyful patience can endure.*

It is the same all through the year. I owe to my
Rectory home the joyful awareness of an eternal sig-
nificance persisting through the swiftly passing beauty
of the seasons. In my mind the Church's year will always
come first. I was born into it. My father and mother
gave it to me. It is entangled in all my thoughts.

Thus to grow up in the Christian year is to learn, in
the words of Thomas Treherne, that 'the World is not
this little cottage of Heaven and Earth, though this be
fair, it is too small a Gift. When God made the world
He made the Heavens, and the Heaven of Heavens,
and the Angels, and the Celestial Powers. These also

are parts of the World: so are all those infinite and eternal Treasures that are to abide for ever, after the Day of Judgement. Neither are these, some here and some there, but all everywhere, and at once to be enjoyed.'

Christmas is not a special prerogative of Rectories. It is 'all everywhere, and at once to be enjoyed'. It belongs to all the world, but when it was over, and we went on through the long dreariness of January, we were companioned by the 'Men of Old' who once followed their star 'with gladness' as they set out on the audacious pilgrimage which sought a king and found a homeless child.

February was marked by Septuagesima Sunday and by my father's reading of the first chapter of Genesis as the Lesson that day, and then we always sang Haydn's anthem, 'The Heavens are telling'. On the following Sunday, there was Newman's hymn, 'Praise to the Holiest in the Height', and then the week when we prayed for 'that most excellent gift of charity'.

It will be seen that our Christian year swung along mainly to the words and tunes of hymns, and they are often a very exciting part of childhood. They recall it for most grown-up people.

The Charity Collect led into Lent, and at Wilton Rectory this season did indeed mean forty days of penance. Between Advent Sunday and Easter Day, my father made a practice of adding to his usual parish visits, a house to house visitation of all the town. He had a passion for statistics, and in the evenings he loved making up his register, inserting full details of every family from year to year. By the time Lent came, he was already tired, and now there were added special services, addresses and instructions, so that he seemed to be hardly ever at home. Lenten dinners were late because of all these services, and Lenten meals were abstemious in character. To add to their dreariness, they were often attended by a visiting preacher, such as Canon Codd, whom my father once wearily asked to 'Have some cod, Codd'. This provoked from the family a furtive lenten grin.

So our pleasures in Lent might be called extremely subdued ones, though there was one which I still remember with peculiar affection. Some of the special services were held in the 'Old church', which was really the chancel of a ruined church standing in the middle of the town. This building was then safe enough to be used, and the services there were much liked by poor people who fancied that their clothes were not grand enough for the parish church. The little chancel was very badly lit, so that shabby hats were not conspicuous, though Mildred and I studied them as well as we could from the choir seats, whence we led Moody and Sankey hymns, to be ardently taken up by the congregation, singing slowly, loudly, and plaintively.

The smell of those services is unforgettable. It was a mixture of flannel, lamp-oil, dripping umbrellas and mackintoshes, mingled with the very old immured damp, which was being drawn by the stoves from the walls, and from the heavy curtains made of red cloth powdered with black fleurs-de-lis.

Over the heads of the congregation, through the

thick smoky air, my eyes always came to rest on the numbers of memorial tablets which covered the walls. To preserve them had been the main reason for the preservation of the chancel when the church was pulled down in 1845. These memorials pointed to a timepiece of yet another type—a timepiece, the pendulum of which beat out the passing of separate human lives, while the family remained. Underlying these eighteenth-century epitaphs was the assumption that though the individuals passed, yet their houses would continue in Wilton and be for ever known there. Some of the tablets contained the records of four or five successive generations in a family of unpretentious burgesses, who had played their parts in the life of the town, as mayors, aldermen, manufacturers, surgeons, or shop-keepers. Their sense of the permanency of the community was not affected by their awareness of the short span of life allotted to each poor mortal. When a man bequeathed a benefit to the town, he decreed that it should continue 'for ever'.

The Phelps family memorial tablet is typical.

'John Phelps. Master of the Free School in this town, died the 21st of November 1823, aged 57. Endowed with qualities of mind and manners that might have graced a higher rank of society, he walked humbly in his own, and at the peaceful close of a tranquil and useful life, he feelingly confessed his own unworthiness, resting all his hope for eternity on the mercy of God, through the merits of his Saviour.

'As Master of the Free School, he succeeded his father, William Phelps, who had conducted it for twenty-eight years, whose virtues he copied, whose memory he tenderly cherished, and with whose ashes his own are now mingled.'

The writer of that epitaph had a great sense of rhythm, and a genius for selecting peacefully-sounding words. The family history is continued to 1878, but by another hand, and with less of music or meaning. In the next generation, 'John Phelps, M.A.' (the University degree suggests a new tradition) 'was for twenty-one years his father's successor in the school'. He died as Vicar of Hatherleigh; while another son of old John Phelps carried 'his qualities of mind and manners to a higher rank of society', and died an Archdeacon and Canon of Carlisle.

The seventeenth-century inscriptions mostly described only the dead man's trade or profession, saying little or nothing of his family. Thomas Mell, for instance, was 'once servante to the Right Honourable William Earle of Pembroke, afterwards to Kinge James and Kinge Charles, and also Mayor of this Borough of Wilton'. He died in 1625; and another tablet commemorates Edmund Phillips, 'Sweeper of Burbidg and Farer to the Earl of Penbruck, hoo died the 19th of January 1677.'

After these, the earliest of the eighteenth-century epitaphs are very tender and touching. Two sisters, Susannah and Mary Bignell, both died in 1726, their ages being eighteen and twenty-three. Of them it is written:

> In the spring and flower of my time,
> My life to God I did resign,

Being in my years so young,
Yet my day was spent, my glass was run.

The Rev. Henry Pitt was evidently a favourite, when he died aged twenty-seven, in 1733.

'His days of nature were as an agreeable tale that is soon told, not tedious, trifling, idle, or insignificant, but short, instructive, moral, and entertaining.'

Poor little Eliuzay Jones must have been a lonely child, with no one very near to lament her when she died. This is her epitaph:

In memory of Eliuzay, a granddaughter of the Rev. Mr. Barford, by Catherine the wife of Mr. Jones of London, who died January 28, 1733, aged 14. Erected by the order of Mr. Sharpe, who died October 28, 1738, aged 71.
'The Righteous shall be had in everlasting remembrance.'

It seems as if the 'righteousness' must refer to Mr. Sharpe who thus parsimoniously ordered a tablet to include his own epitaph with that of little Eliuzay.

In a very dark corner was the almost-obliterated tablet to the memory of John Hickey Gent, who 'deceased ye 25th of March Ano 1709. On it I thought I read the words:

'Earth lies on thy heart,' followed by more which was illegible, till a candle disclosed what was less poetical though hardly less ominous. The inscription really ran thus:

Reader, write on thy heart and still bear it in mind, the Wicked go into everlasting punishment, the righteous into life eternal.

Of Robert Powell Whitmarsh, surgeon and apothecary and alderman of this borough, one of the Coroners for the County, who died in 1829, aged fifty-seven, it is written:

> *The summons came while yet life's onward stage*
> *He walked, not worn by sickness, nor by age*
> *Dust sank to dust: th'unbodied spirit's eye*
> *Saw—Reader! ask not what, but learn to die.*
> *Found if well sought, seek early thou, and find*
> *Pardon in Christ, in pardon, peace of mind.*
> *So shalt thou stand when life's worst ills arise,*
> *Nor be 'found sleeping' at the Great Surprise.*

By this time, the piety of the earlier epitaphs was turning to didacticism, but in the eighteenth century, when the writers dwelt unflinchingly on the dust to which all men were doomed to return and when the sculptors depicted urns, hour-glasses, skeletons, and other emblems now sometimes considered 'pagan'—the message of the epitaphs was unshakenly Christian. They taught a tender calm.

The tablet I looked at most often was to the memory of 'Caroline Letitia Hetley, wife of Richard Hetley, Esq., who died universally loved and lamented on the 25th of November 1829, aged twenty-nine years.'

Thirty years later, another epitaph had been added, that of Richard Hetley himself, of whom it was only said that he died in his seventy-fourth year, 'the widower of the above Caroline Letitia'.

Lent ended at last, even at Wilton Rectory. In the two months from mid-April to midsummer, the beauty of nature is intoxicating. Each day seems to be the loveliest of all. But however much one revels simply in

[124]

the flowery glory of those weeks, they must always for me fall into their place in the Christian year. A radiance falls upon the earth from the celestial festivals of Easter, Ascension Day, and Whit-Sunday, as light drips from the stars upon the quiet fields. Snow may fall on Easter Sunday, and indeed it often does, yet the Easter hymns do not fail to awake the very soul of spring. When Ascension Day comes, the thin young green on the trees carries the heart upward through it to the sky; and Whit-Sunday always seems to be the most beautiful day in the year. As a child I was taught that the Day of Pentecost was the Birthday of the Church: it is also the birthday of millions of flowers.

Undeniably there were times when the discipline of the Christian year, as administered by my father, did chafe on the young. These things were for him not only the chief things in the world—they were the only things. And he demanded that they should be this for everyone else. That complete singleness of mind was the secret of his influence. After a vain protest against a Field Day for Volunteers which was held on Good Friday, he resigned his Commission as Chaplain to the Fourth Wilts; and for years he fought a losing battle with the Jockey Club in the endeavour to change the date of Salisbury Races, held on Ascension Day. On such points he would not compromise.

Equally, he would never allow his daughters to be away from home on any of the great Church festivals. It was our duty to keep them in our own parish church. This cut out many pleasures, and we often rebelled inwardly. But my father's system was like Mr. Street's.

It 'swept you round and round with it'; and as it did
so, it left with you something greater than yourself
which was to remain through life.

WITHOUT KNOWING ME. WALKLEY

IX

★ POOR PEOPLE ★

Poor people were terribly poor when I was a child.
Mrs. Jeffery was one of the poorest. She 'lived on' the
parish, or rather, she received from the Guardians a
weekly allowance of half a crown and a loaf of bread,
the under part of which she sold, every week, for two-
pence, to a neighbour who had a large family of children. She paid a rent of two shillings a week for her
house in Fancy Row, an L-shaped group of quite well-
built houses dating from early in the last century. They
stood off the street, round a piece of garden land. Her
sitting-room was of a good size, and was well-propor-
tioned, as rooms in the smallest houses still were at
that date. Here she sat, facing life on eightpence a week
and the top of a loaf. Her case was not exceptional. Hers
was the usual allowance given to a solitary woman; and
probably the Guardians hoped, by means of this eco-
nomic pressure, to induce the poor lonely old things
to go into the Workhouse. There, even in those days,
they would have been cared for as they never could be
in their own homes, but they one and all dreaded the
prospect. However few and valueless one's personal

belongings may be, they make the familiar setting of
one's life; and it is hard that the world should prema-
turely bring home to one that 'we brought nothing
into this world, neither may we carry anything out',
especially when it invites us to leave this world, not
for a Heavenly Mansion, but for an 'Institution'. It
must seem like a first and agonizing death thus to be
torn from all one's little treasures; and everyone collects
a few of these in the course of a long life, even though
it may be a long life of unbroken poverty.

Mrs. Jeffery's neighbour, for instance, Mrs. Wilkins,
lived in equal penury, and apparently had always done
so, yet both her dress and her cottage indicated that, if
she had been born in another sphere, she would have
been a dilettante collector of *objets d'art*. Her thin bony
form was clothed in the most poverty-stricken garments, but she draped them about her person in the
arty manner of the 'eighties, fastening them here and
there with baroque brooches and buckles, while her
meagre arms tinkled with bracelets. Round the bent
and broken brim of her dilapidated hat, she tossed a
fluttering blue veil, through which she peered at her
visitors with bleary, half-blind eyes. Her dirty little
room was a museum. Its walls were covered with her
collection of jugs. She possessed hundreds of these—a
mixed and motley jumble, none of them of much beauty
or value; yet they ensured for their owner a happy variety of colours, shapes, and memories, upon which to
rest her worn-out eyes. This storehouse of rather dirty
antiques was no doubt a less hygienic abode for Mrs.
Wilkins's declining years than would have been a ward

at the Workhouse, with its clean sanitary walls; and yet, who would hesitate if asked to choose between the two?

Lean as she was, Mrs. Wilkins looked less starved than Mrs. Jeffery, so that possibly at some time in her life she had been better nourished. She had perhaps been in service in some house where she acquired her artistic tastes. Mrs. Jeffery, on the other hand, had always eked out a poor living by part-time labour on a farm. She had often slung across her shoulders the baby she was nursing at the time, while she ran up to the fields for a few hours' weeding or hoeing; or she had gleaned a few ears of corn to be ground into flour by the miller. At eighty years of age, she frequently told us of a red-letter day in her life when, as a little girl, she had gone to tea at the farmhouse, and had been given 'real butter'.

Mrs. Jeffery once came to see me in great distress.

'I've 'ad a misfartune,' she said. 'I've a-broke me po, and 'e was such a beautiful po. 'E 'adn't got ne'er an 'andle, but 'e 'ad a very nice rim. 'E wer old Mr. Rawlence's po, and when I did use to go up there to mend the carpet, I did see this po, and I allers liked un. And then, when I 'ad me fire and all me things was burnt, Master Freddy Rawlence brought un down to me, and I've a 'ad un ever since.'

We both felt very shy at the idea of going into a shop, to replace this indispensable piece of property, but at last I faced a lady shopkeeper who promised to 'pack it invisibly', as they say.

Yet, in spite of Mrs. Jeffery and Mrs. Wilkins, we

often remarked in those old days that there was little acute poverty in Wilton. This sounds incredible in face of the actual incomes of these old women, but although I have told the truth about their allowances, that is not the whole truth. Wilton was and is a small place, and in those days at least, we made a family party. Nobody sat down to a hot joint for dinner, without making sure that at least one of their poorer neighbours was doing the same. Every day, in the streets of Wilton, we saw, between twelve and one, three or four of the pony carriages in which old ladies were then in the habit of taking the air. These were low basket-shaped vehicles containing two seats which faced each other. The owner of the carriage usually held the reins, with another lady seated at her side. If there was a third member of the party, this rather unlucky person was perched on the opposite seat, ducking her head and trying to avoid the reins which were passed over her shoulder. The pony-carriages I speak of contained Mrs. Rawlence, Mrs. Naish, and Miss Nightingale, and during those pre-luncheon drives, the front seats were usually stacked with baskets containing basins. In these were slices of meat cut off the steaming joints, and surrounded by vegetables and gravy. But people without pony-carriages were about the same business at the same time; and my early memories of the Wilton streets about the hour of noon, show them peopled with women running into each other's houses, carrying steaming basins covered with cloths.

In those days there was a good deal of drunkenness in the country, and this was a distress to old Mrs. Rawlence. Still, she was well aware that on Sundays, when the public-houses were shut, the men would miss their pint of beer, and might feel depressed. Mrs. Rawlence remembered the Children of Israel who picked up a double portion of manna before the Sabbath Day, and so Saturday was her greatest day for driving about. She went to the drunkards' houses bringing them jugs of strong coffee and of delicious and very concentrated *consommé*. Thus she hoped, not only to minister to the thirst of the coming day, but also to suggest that other drinks might always take the place of beer.

When Mrs. Rawlence died, her husband endowed a Wilton Parish Nurse, thinking mainly of the old people who would miss the kind friend visiting them in their poverty. Nurse Turner filled this post to perfection. Hers is one of the unforgettable Wilton figures. She was a tall woman, with an affectionate rolling gait, and an expression of calm beneficence. She always carried a round basket in her hand, and in summer she wore, instead of her nurse's bonnet, a very wide white straw hat. She was a liaison officer between those people in Wilton who had enough and to spare, and those who didn't know how to make ends meet. She was equally at home in the houses of both sorts, and she knew people's possessions better than they knew them themselves. She came into a house, with her quiet deaf smile, to ask for the loan of 'the drinking-cup on the top shelf of your china cupboard', for 'those warm woollen slippers that your dear mother found such a comfort when she was ill', or for 'the hatbox that came with your hat from Style and Gerrish, which I could use to make a cradle over a little boy's broken leg'. People were delighted to know that their treasures had been observed by Nurse Turner, and also that they could so easily do something to give comfort to a sick neighbour.

This 'Lady Bountiful' system is discountenanced to-day, and of course it could never have touched the fringe of the poverty in large industrial towns; but in Wilton we all knew each other well and were naturally neighbourly without any touch of patronage or of pauperizing.

Past generations of Wilton people took their part in supplementing the inadequate Poor Relief of those days. Wilton is rich in old 'Charities', bequests made by eighteenth century weavers or other manufacturers, to provide schooling, marriage portions, old age pensions, and almshouses for poor people in Wilton. Thus the prosperity of the town two hundred years ago overflows into to-day.

Then there was the Church. The Wilton Almshouses are mostly the modern forms of medieval priories and hospitals, of which there were many in the town, and the spirit of their founders has lived on. Out-relief was at first only an allowance supplementary to the charity of Christian people, and certainly Wilton congregations never thought their responsibilities over when they had paid their rates. My father, as Rector, made it his personal care that no one in his parish should be without a fire; and every month the Church people subscribed largely for the 'Sick and Poor'. This money was chiefly distributed by District Visitors in the form of food tickets.

So no one was quite forgotten in Wilton when they were in difficulties; yet, however well these funds were spent, life must have been a precarious affair for Mrs. Jeffery and her friends. To-day, old age pensions are paid on a more adequate scale than the Poor Relief of my youth, and the Guardians augment them too with grants towards the rent. The recipients are 'independent'. The 'half-crown and a loaf' have gone for ever. There are few things which I did at Wilton which gave me more pleasure at the time than the immense task of copying Baptismal Registers, which was handed over to me by my father in 1908. In that year, old people of seventy received their first Old Age Pensions of five shillings a week. But they were first called upon to prove their ages, and for years after 1838, birth certificates did not exist. You could only prove that you had been born by proving that you had been baptized, and the unfortunate thing was that some of these old people found that they had not been christened till they were four or five years old. Their parents sometimes took them to church in batches. Though some of them could remember scampering round the Font on the day of the baptism, that did not count as evidence. Documentary proof was essential, and documentary proof meant the Parish Registers. This experience shook my faith in the relative value of written and of traditional evidence in all matters of history. Still, the Pensions authorities demanded copies of the Register; and if some early nineteenth-century parents had been dilatory over the admission of their children to the Church, the Sins of the Fathers were now visited on the septuagenarian

[133]

children, who were not seventy in the eyes of the law till seventy years after their belated entry into the Church.

For many years, the Relieving Officer at Wilton was Mr. Wiles, a bustling little man with a kind heart and a sense of justice. He achieved the difficult combination of kindness to the poor with fairness to the ratepayers. He was entirely familiar with the resources of the families under his care, and he always knew when people could not live on the allowance granted them. Then he got more for them, either from the Guardians or from the Church. On the other hand, he was most severe on people who tried to throw dust in his eyes by making false statements, and he once said to me, about a very eccentric old woman:

'Have you ever noticed anything peculiar about the shape of Patty's chest?'

I modestly denied it.

'I have then,' said Mr. Wiles. 'It's my belief that she's got a silver teapot in there. I know she had one once, and I don't know what has become of it. Some day, I shall take hold of it and give it a shake.'

I don't know whether he ever took this desperate step; but if Patty really had a teapot in her bust, its shape must have been 'peculiar' enough to give her away without any shaking.

Mr. Wiles could always be relied on to turn a blind eye if he chanced to pass the cottage of one of his old women at the moment when one of the ladies of the town was carrying in a chicken to be plucked, or a piece of needlework to be done. Anyone who thus earned a

few pence to augment her weekly allowance of two
shillings and elevenpence (without the loaf) was liable
to have it withdrawn altogether; but if Mr. Wiles knew
nothing about it, of course he couldn't report it to the
Guardians. These august personages themselves would
look over the head of Mrs. Jeffery when she happened
to be mending a carpet in a house belonging to one of
them; for Guardians and Relieving Officers alike knew
the difference made by the earning of those few for-
bidden pence.

The lovely word Charity is out of favour to-day; and
the personal gifts which brightened the days I write of,
are now looked back on as ugly symptoms of a state of
society in which the rich alternately trampled upon, and
patronized, the poor. Yet the unhappy people in those
days were those who lived in big towns out of reach
of this simple and friendly giving and receiving. In
little country places, these presents often passed between people whose circumstances were not actually
very far apart; and they carried with them a personal
friendship which an Income-Tax return cannot convey.
The columns of figures which fill our Rates and Taxes
Demand Notes have taken the place of the basins which
used to bring dinners from one house to another, and
a great deal of flavour is lost in this exchange.

X

★ SCENES AND SAYINGS ★

'Talking about talking'—with this arresting phrase, I once heard old Mr. Rawlence cut his way into a conversation which was not about talking at all. I had certainly been chattering more than was seemly on the part of a young girl in the presence of her elders, and it was time for a well-earned snub, as well as for the company to hear Mr. Rawlence speak.

Talking is, however, quite a good subject for conversation, and I like to remember good talks in the past, or even isolated phrases. I often find in my old diaries, a telling phrase I heard, or a little picture I saw, written down with no context, and I can remember nothing else about them. Yet those passages make my diary worth while. They interrupt the record of every day, with its inevitable everyday-ness.

Mrs. Stephen Musselwhite bubbled with phrases and was a rattling good talker. Every time one went to see her, she threw off something which was worth jotting down. Her neighbours called her 'False Emma'; but, as she said: 'Folks say I'm proud, but I'm not. I just don't care about talking to anyone but you, and the

Saviour, and the Clutterbucks.' She was as fastidious about books as about the company she kept, and she returned a book which had been lent to her saying: 'No thank you. I only like *good* books, about God and death.'

'That's my slop basin,' she called out recklessly, as she gave herself another cup of tea, and threw into the grate the tea leaves from her first cup; and then she turned to me with an appraising look, and said: 'You're little and desperate. You ought to marry a lord with a thousand a year.'

One of her sons emigrated to Canada, where he bought a farm, and my father said he was glad to hear he had fallen on his feet.

'Fallen on his feet?' said Mrs. Musselwhite, indignant. 'Indeed he hasn't. He rides a 'orse.'

A few years later, this son died in Canada, and Mrs. Musselwhite who, as we know, liked 'God and death' was much consoled by hearing of the 'Glass 'earse' which was used at the funeral. 'Something better'n what we 'as 'ere,' she said. She was rather puzzled when she heard that the funeral had taken place some way from the farm, and she decided that her son 'must have lived in a little country place just outside Canada, much like Barford is to Wilton.'

Mrs. Strong was another phrase-maker, and she said scornfully of a somewhat feckless neighbour whose child had died:

'I 'ad to do everything for her this morning. She couldn't so much as lay out a cat, as the saying is.'

Excited speakers at Suffragette meetings have been known to let fall some unexpected utterances.

'I don't stand before you as a *woman*,' declared a rather peculiarly dressed female speaker on the Market Cross at Wilton one day. She then condoled with those unfortunate women 'whose nearest male relative is a MAN', and defiantly demanded—'No Taxation without Legislation'.

In those same pre-war days of Suffrage debate, I once heard Lady Robert Cecil (herself an ardent Suffragist) say impatiently, on hearing that a publisher had refused Walter de la Mare's Nursery Rhymes as 'unsuitable for children':

'I suppose they sent it to be read by some idiotic woman.'

Whereat Sir Henry Newbolt took her ear-trumpet and said gravely down it:

'Not a case for giving women the vote then?'

At a missionary meeting, the speaker declared fervently: 'I believe—in fact I *know*—that there will be black men in Heaven. They want to go there as much as we do, but they don't know the way. WE DO.'

It was, however, neither the salvation of black men, nor votes for women, but a friendly tea-party for Sunday School teachers which brought forth this, said very rapidly:

'I didn't hear direct, but I heard sideways, and I wished the earth would sink and open me up.'

Miss Aikman then asked the meaning of the word 'Bounder', which she had heard used about one of her friends.

No one was quite sure as to this, but everyone agreed that it was something complimentary.

This scrap of conversation is very unintelligible:

He said: 'How's your mother?'

I said, *most* sarcastically: 'Quite well thank you.'

But that delicate sarcasm has evaporated.

For many years we had at the Rectory a most inspired gardener named Chalke. He was not a great talker, but if anyone ever had the Green Thumb, it was he. The garden was his one thought. He could not live away from it, and on summer evenings, when we were at dinner with the windows open, we never failed to see Old Chalke come back from his cottage, to slip through the garden gate for a last prowl round his flower beds. He was like a mother who shades her candle with her hand as she steals into the night nursery to see that the little ones are safely asleep.

When my sister once showed Old Chalke a particularly delightful photograph she had taken of the garden, he looked at it for some time with his 'fat affectionate smile', and said:

'Wheelbarrer comes out jolly.'

There was poetry in Chalke's last words. He had got up at five one morning, and was smoking a pipe by the window, when he said meditatively to his wife:

'We've had a lovely rain. Do 'ee hear that blackbird whistling?'

She heard a sudden movement and looked towards him. The old gardener was sitting dead in his chair while the blackbird whistled.

Remembered scenes are often scenes of choirs, for choirs naturally make pictures. I wish I had seen the old west gallery choirs—trombones, flutes, and the round mouths of singing girls; and still more I wish I heard them oftener now, the music floating freely down from above, and compelling the congregation to join. There is lovely singing of this kind in the little village Church of Untergrainau not far from Oberammergau, where on any Sunday it seems as if every person in the church was breaking into spontaneous and rapturous devotion in the music of Bach or of Handel, and this entirely because the choir is behind them. I heard something of the same sort at a wedding in Woodford Church in Wiltshire.

Choir practices are often more delightful to see than to hear. As children we were sometimes allowed to be present at a special anthem practice which was held once a month in the church before Sunday Evensong. Ordinary practices were in the School or Church Room, but anthems had a final polish *in situ*. We sat at the far end of the dark church, and the only lights were the romantic gas flares from the old Italian hanging lamps in the choir. It looked like a scene on the stage. The choir wore cassocks, the boys with white frills round their necks, and a cassocked clergyman watched the proceedings. Perhaps it was the gaslight above and the dark cassocks below which made the faces of the singers look abnormally white.

After some preliminary stamping and walking about, the choir burst forth into what sounded in the empty church to be the most glorious singing in the world. It was a well-known chorus from the Messiah, and the singers let themselves go with complete certainty. But every few bars, this joyous *abandon* was interrupted by the organist taking his hands off the keys and clapping them smartly. The basses were always enjoying themselves with such tremendous force, that they sang on for several bars before they realized that they had been left in the air without support from the organ. When they stopped, at last, there came an angry shouting voice from the side of the chancel. From where we heard it, it had a doubled, echoing sound. Mr. Ridley, the organist, was expressing his horror at the discords which had sounded to us so magnificent; and the choir had to 'Go back to Letter A'. There was a flutter of paper, and then they sang again. No music has ever had for me quite the same quality as those Handel choruses, swinging boldly along, sharply interrupted, and then gradually falling to pieces, one voice breaking off after another, till a solitary tenor was left suspended on a high note, quite out of his reach, from which he suddenly came down in panic.

When I taught the choir at Netherhampton, our practices were far more primitive. We met in the very small school of this little hamlet, and the members of the choir doubled their legs under them, and squatted on the Infants' benches. There were no lamps, and as it grew dark, each man lit his own candle and held it near his book. It made an enchanting scene. There was old Dimmer the Ploughman, with his grandly carved face, his grey beard and thick grey hair, and the patient humorous eyes which are often seen in men who spend their lives in watching the earth and the sky. Dimmer could read a few words, but no music. He learnt the words of the hymns at the practice, while he extemporized a perfectly harmonious bass which he sang in a full musical voice. Toomer, a gentle furtive man with a black beard, said he liked to 'sing air' but he stammered so badly that he had hardly ever begun to sing before the hymn was over. Mr. Cox was a very grand musician, who had sung in a town choir, and who looked on us all as rather despicable amateurs, while Mrs. Terrill, with her pretty complexion and fair hair, did not make much noise, but always came because she liked to support the Church. Then there was Dorothy Hayden, who could easily have carried the service on her own shoulders if no one else came at all. She was our only real singer; and she was a rock in the midst of the usual little group of shuffling children which completed our choir.

If I was away, Mr. Tutt, the churchwarden, sometimes took charge with such enterprise as to disconcert the rest of the choir completely. Old Dimmer came to me one day in tears because Mr. Tutt had changed the music on Sunday, so that he 'knew no more about it than that tree, and couldn't sing all through the service, but just stood up there looking silly'.

Candles are the perfect light for choirs, as anyone will agree who remembers a service in Magdalen Chapel at Oxford, or in King's College, Cambridge. There is a week in the year when Evensong begins by daylight, the rich colours of the medieval glass glowing behind the heads of the choristers. Then darkness creeps up, those colours turn to ashes, and there springs to life, beside each singer, a thin white flame which has really been lit all the time. Those lines of surpliced figures, and the row of pointed flames have a very chaste beauty.

Never can I forget a Choral Festival in Salisbury Cathedral when great clusters of banners—thirty or forty at once—were grouped together at intervals in the procession of choirs. They appeared from the light outside the West Door, and surged up and down over the steps into the nave, swaying and bending as they came under the porch, and making a confused and moving sea of colour. Their restless shadows fell upon the faces of choirboys who moved along, their eyes on their books, singing very earnestly. Every time those banners moved under the high austere pointed arches, the effect was miraculous. Then came a moment when they were all held rigid and aloft, while the massed choirs stood before the altar to sing 'Ein Feste Burg'. Far away at the east end, Bishop Ridgeway stood like a small statue in his mitre and cope of cloth of gold. My father, who saw things vividly, said that he looked like a chess bishop, and he did.

XI

I suppose that in those old days my father was the most outstanding character in Wilton, and he is very difficult to describe. He was like a force of nature, moulding one's life, and yet never a part of it. He was too important to be that. The immense force and impetus of his personality came largely from the fact that for years he had disciplined himself to live by unalterable rules which extended to his every action from the least to the greatest. Even his meals were significant. They never varied, when he was at home, and, perhaps for that very reason, he went away less and less. For breakfast, he had two fillets of sole, two pieces of toast and marmalade, and two cups of cocoa-nibs: for luncheon, two mutton chops and two baked apples: for tea, two slices of bread and butter: at night, two cigarettes. At dinner he allowed some variety, but this was not an exception to his rule: it was a part of the rule, which laid down that the evening was a time for a sedate and well-regulated social life.

His days were exactly planned. Matins in the church at eight: breakfast at eight-thirty: leave the house at eight-forty-five (after which we had family prayers without him): prayers in the chapel at Wilton House at nine, and so on throughout the day. He enjoyed thus to dovetail his work, including in his day a good number of fixed engagements between which he fitted the many unexpected demands which are made on the time of a country parson.

From this record of my father's day, he might appear easy to know—a mere man of routine. Yet this is far from the case. The routine was on the surface: it had been deliberately assumed: beneath the uniformity was a man of quite another type.

My father used to tell us that when he left Oxford, he decided that he disliked his handwriting, which was ugly, irregular, and illegible. He therefore changed it, making it firm, clear, and very balanced. So it remained. This too was himself.

There were in my father two people—the natural man, and the man formed by reason, judgment, and a religion based on the Church Catechism, and centred round the duty towards God, and the duty towards my neighbour. He did not ask from the faith which he so firmly kept, any mystical consolations: he demanded a definite line of conduct. Probably the fundamental traits in a character are never wholly obliterated, but by the time I knew my father, the Old Adam in him had become as completely sublimated as was his handwriting. He had adapted himself to the mould which he had made.

His Latin blood equipped him with a disposition which was active, lively, witty, artistic, and amusing.

He was musical, highly strung, sensitive, and nervous. A small light figure, he won many a steeplechase at Christ Church, and distinguished himself at Oxford in the game of 'real' tennis, as he always called it. He hunted a great deal, and was an extremely good shot. He loved travel, knowing the small towns of Italy as well as the great celebrated places; and his walking tours with Oxford friends made him acquainted with all parts of the Highlands as well as the English Lake Country.

After becoming a clergyman, he gradually gave up all these pursuits, not, at first, because he thought them wrong (though he did ultimately almost think that they were) but because he was resolved to give every faculty he possessed, every ounce of energy, every moment of time, to the service of the Church. The swift firm steps carried him now no farther than the limits of his beloved parish: his sporting clothes were exchanged for clerical attire which was, even in those days, ultracorrect: the slim figure which he had delighted to keep down to 'Derby weight' became, without adding an ounce of weight, that 'commanding presence' which made Lady Pembroke declare that she always thought him 'taller than George', her husband of six feet six in height. Nobody would have guessed that he was to the end of his life an extremely nervous man, for he had taught himself an unshakable composure of manner, and could handle a difficult meeting, or face an unexpected emergency with unruffled ease.

Such self-control can only be achieved, as the Bible says: 'by prayer and fasting', and it must have cost my father a great deal of both. When he first came to Wilton, he still hunted occasionally with the Blackmore Vale, and kept a hunter at Sherborne; he shot frequently with the young Herberts; he played lawn-tennis two or three times a week with his curates. Then he found that all these things were taking him away from the work of his life, and by degrees they were all given up. To the last, he was completely at home when he got on to a horse, but he never kept one after he became Rector of Wilton. Only once do I remember his even contemplating the idea of shooting, and then he accepted a most tempting invitation to shoot grouse with a cousin in Scotland. He packed his guns, and started for the station. On the way, he thought he ought not to go, and he turned back and came home. But though for years he never shot, he did not lose his eye, and I remember once when we were children, we looked with him across a little stream at the end of the garden at the poultry field of a smallholder. Running about among the chickens was a huge rat. Papa sped back to the house and brought his gun. Then he climbed up on to a paling, and holding the gun at a most difficult angle, he picked out that rat among all the bustling chickens, and it rolled over dead amidst a chorus of squawks from the hens.

Gardening was a recreation he allowed himself, for though it was a pleasure, it was also 'working in the garden'. He and my mother looked supremely happy and serene on summer evenings when she sat on her camp-stool beside him while he weeded, and a robin usually perched on the handle of the weeding-basket.

Sometimes when he was reading or writing in the

study, with the forbidding label '*Engaged*' hung outside, the door would suddenly be found open, and the room empty. He had sprung up, and gone out to bud a rose. This he always found complete refreshment when his head was tired.

As life went on, my father became more and more austere, and he expected his family to become so with him. Nay more, he insisted that they should, and he was very autocratic. Looking back now upon that life, which my father's determination of character had built into so logical and definite an achievement, one feels for it only an immense and wholehearted admiration, yet candour compels the admission that he was at times extremely difficult to live with. He expected his sons and daughters to adopt his own peculiar rule of life, and he used no persuasion to dispose them to this. He commanded. Probably there is never comfortable elbow-room in a house for more than one idealist.

My father, who enjoyed conversation, and was himself a very good talker, lost much of the pleasure of this most agreeable art because everyone coming into the house seemed to know by instinct that nothing must be spoken of, of which he did not approve. This limited the range of conversation at his table. If he could once have admitted a greater freedom, he would soon have enjoyed it very much, but he was as rigid in this as in other things. His mind had been made up. Within his self-imposed limits, he was a delightful and sparkling conversationalist—witty, vivid, and picturesque. Living with him was great fun when he allowed it to be so.

The many interesting people we met at Wilton House
in those days cannot fairly be called 'Wilton Characters', yet they made the character of the place in which
we grew up. George Lord Pembroke and Gety his
wife were very remarkable people, and to Wilton came
most of the interesting men and women of the day.
Lord Pembroke was the most beautiful being I ever
saw—beautiful alike in person and in spirit. He was
immensely tall, with a small head, a short dark beard,
and wonderful Russian eyes which were set in his head
at a curious drooping angle. He walked with steps
which seemed too short for the length of his legs, and
this gave to his carriage a manner of bewitching
modesty. He was a man of great intellectual power
with deep, sad thoughts, and a rare sense of nonsense
and of fun. Disraeli had made him an under-secretary
of State at the age of twenty-three, and must have seen
in him one of the romantic, aristocratic, political
dreamers of his own early novels. But by then Lord
Pembroke had already lived more than half of his short
life, and his health quickly broke down under the strain
of politics. Disraeli's insight was justified however, for
Wilton now became a country house such as he depicted in *Lothair*, filled with a succession of statesmen,
travellers, artists, writers, and beautiful women.

Like more than one of his predecessors, Lord Pembroke married a Talbot, and Lady Pembroke was a
woman of magnificent appearance. She was tall and
very dignified, and her figure was well adapted to the
brocades and the elaborate dresses of her day. She wore
them splendidly, and somehow she succeeded in re-

maining very dignified even when her very long thick hair of pale chestnut colour fell in loops upon her neck, as it often did. The Pembrokes were very advanced for the times in which they lived, for they both walked about the country without hats, so that many of their neighbours thought them quite mad. Lord Pembroke used to walk thus for miles about the estate, dropping in at one of the down farms for a bit of bread and cheese, and sometimes finding that he had walked so far from home that he had to borrow half a crown from his farmer host to take him back to Wilton by train. It is curious to remember that in those days, before telephones and motor cars, a walk of fifteen miles on one's own estate could end in marooning one quite out of reach of the household and horses one had left behind a few hours before.

It was also possible to lose oneself on Salisbury Plain in a carriage. Lady Pembroke used to take us for drives in a phaeton and pair with a groom perched up behind, and we drove for miles over the turf where there were no roads and no sign of human habitation. The huge horizon enfolded a vast circle of green undulations, and there were often no landmarks in sight for many miles. Lady Pembroke loved this, and we used to drive on and on, stopping at intervals for the groom to stand up in his seat and scour the country with his eyes till he saw something—a clump of trees, or a barn—which gave him his bearings, and then we knew where we were.

Lady Pembroke always did what came into her head. She planted ivy all over the park, training it upon the

trunks of the trees, and refusing to believe that anything so slender could possibly harm the forest trees
which it so gracefully throttled. When she could no
longer bear the shabbiness of Katie Thynne's old hat,
she threw it into the fire before us all, and gave her a
wonderful new one the next day; and her sympathy
with the lobsters caught by a party in the yacht, com-
pelled her to throw them back into the sea, although
their scarlet shells proclaimed that they had already
been boiled. Once, when Lady Pembroke was sitting
talking with my mother at the Rectory, the gardener
began to mow a narrow strip of grass outside the window. The machine kept starting and stopping and
starting again, and it made an irritating fidgety noise.
My mother, who was accustomed to writing letters
to the accompaniment of five-finger exercises played on
the piano, ignored this in her calm disciplined way. Not
so Lady Pembroke. She sprang to her feet, and with
her fingers in her ears, she ran to the window and
leaned out, crying: 'Stop! Stop!! STOP!!!'

Mamma thought this extremely uncontrolled.

Lady Pembroke's waywardness made her often alarming. She invited us to tea, and then forgot all about it,
and when we arrived she begged us to go away. Sometimes she was seized with the whim of dressing one of
us up in some fantastic ridiculous dress, to appear as a
caller, as a practical joke on another guest, and she
would allow no refusal. There were days when she
allowed us to talk recklessly and disrespectfully about
our elders, for she loved to be amused; but then she
often repented, and wrote a touching humble letter

telling us that we had been wrong, and she still more wrong to listen.

Lord Pembroke's three sisters were all married to remarkable men. Lady Mary was the wife of Baron Freddy von Hügel, perhaps the profoundest Christian thinker of his day. He was very deaf, and his talk was an amazing jumble of German philosophical terms and of schoolboy slang. He used whichever vocabulary most nearly approached the fresh original thought which he was flashing out from the caverns of his spirit. Being with him was like going into King Solomon's Mines. Lady Maud's husband was Hubert Parry the composer —a whirlwind of genius. He loved outdoor sports, and most of all, dangerous ones. His family at last refused to sail with him in his little yacht off the Sussex coast, as he preferred these excursions far more when they ended with a capsize and a swim home. Lady Maud declared that in his early days as a motorist, he 'always came home covered with blood', and I remember his skating on the Rectory pond when, in the midst of an elaborate figure, he fell in, the ice cracking in all directions. All the other skaters fled to the bank, and there sat Hubert Parry, as if he was in his bath, and looking extremely jolly and happy, head, feet and arms supported on the ominously cracking ice. He quickly jumped out and ran dripping to the kitchen, from whence he returned with a red-hot salamander. With this he melted down all the jagged pieces of ice, so that the skating the next day should not be spoilt.

Lady Maud's great beauty was ravaged by ill-health and completely ignored by herself. Her extremely dilapidated clothes were hung on her anyhow, but her appearance continued to be most distinguished, while the sudden flash of her smile, and the brilliant glance of her magnificent eyes, gave great rarity to her beauty. She loved teasing, and it was often really for the pleasure of teasing somebody that she first embraced the 'Causes' which she adopted. Nothing delighted her more than to gaze proudly at some conventional acquaintance as she marched by in a Suffragette procession.

Lord Pembroke's youngest sister was that dazzling woman Lady Ripon, whose husband was distinguished too, for he was the best shot in the country. Unlike her sisters, Lady Ripon was a great figure in Society. She was recognized as a social queen in most European capitals, and at Wilton I chiefly remember the gaiety of her laughter. She hid us in her bedroom when Lady Pembroke had told us to go home, and there we watched her being dressed for dinner by Ellen Mitchell, her old nurse, who lived in the town, and who came every evening to see her when she was at Wilton. I think that, to the end of her life, Lady Ripon loved Ellen more than anyone else.

In the town of Wilton lived many interesting people. Near by the semicircular wall and gateway of stone and brick which faces the church, and makes so charming an entrance to the school, is a building containing the two houses of the head teachers. In my early years, one of these was occupied by Mr. Corby with his wife and family, and the other by Miss Sargent. Mr. Corby was a Cornishman, and the Head Master of the Boys'

School. He looked as if he was made entirely of bone, even to the texture of his hard black hair, and his short pointed beard. His large aquiline nose was fierce, and when he smiled, the smile seemed only to be a rather difficult movement of his lower jaw. Mr. Corby's old pupils had a great respect and affection for him, but at first sight, I never saw a sterner face than his. That smile in the jaw was nearly always cut short by the firm black beard. His personality was like his native county, that harsh Cornish moorland, slate-coloured and forbidding, yet haunted by sudden appearances of those Celtic Leprechauns which are like no other kind of fairy. Such were the odd dark gleams of fun which sometimes crossed Mr. Corby's face.

The tin mine which had belonged to his family was derelict, as are many others in the county, and Mr. Corby never seemed to go home. Perhaps he had no relations left there. This dark man had come up alone from the land of Celtic twilight, though he himself was more like a Celtic night, black and sinister. Yet he possessed an unexpected charm: his was the quality of chicory which is both crisp and bitter.

Mr. Corby was no musician, but on the Tuesday in Holy Week it was the custom for the Head Master of the Boys' School to play the harmonium at the morning service in the church. The children of the various schools took turns to form the choir during that week, the head teachers accompanying them. Mr. Corby would not let down the boy's school by sending a substitute organist. He may not have been musical, but he was acute. His choice of hymns was limited

[154]

to those appropriate to Holy Week, yet among these
he discovered one which can be so interpreted as to
be easier to play than any other hymn in the book.
He played it unfailingly every year for at least fifteen
years, and no one recognized this except ourselves.
The hymn was 'Glory be to Jesus', and this is the tune:

The notes lie anyhow under the hand, but Mr. Corby
cleverly simplified it still further. By turning most of
the crotchets into minims, he could reduce to seven
the number of notes in each half of the tune. This was
his version:

When Mr. Corby played over his interpretation of the tune, it carried with it a kind of shorthand or telegraphic suggestion of the words, thus:

> *Glor be Jee*
> *Who bitter pains*
> *Pour me life*
> *From sacred veins.*

He pressed his hands on the keys and blew vigorously while the boys sang lustily, for he had practised them well in advance. The tune too is quite easy to sing when accompanied in this manner.

An unbroken feud existed between Mr. Corby and his neighbour Miss Sargent, the Head of the Girls' School. Their two doors were barely six inches apart, and at the same hour on each day, these doors opened simultaneously for the two teachers to pass to their respective schools. Later on they returned simultaneously to their houses. Yet they hated each other so much that for fifteen years they never spoke except on ceremonial public occasions. Hers was a very different character to his. She had the grace in living which he lacked. As a girl, she must have been very pretty, and she and her sisters (who often visited her) retained to middle life considerable personal charm. Miss Sargent was immensely interested in human nature. The study of character absorbed her, and also the daily events of other people's lives. She loved people, whether they were her pupils, her assistant teachers, her neighbours, or the friends and relations of any of these. She knew all about the Queen and the Royal Family, as well as the public men and women of the day. She enjoyed gossip and always had plenty to tell. She loved her garden, and even more she loved wild flowers. On Shrove Tuesday, when the schools had a half-holiday, Miss Sargent always took us as children for a walk to a far-off spur of Grovely Wood. There she knew she would always find the first primroses. Never was winter so long or spring so lagging that she failed to find at least some tiny buds hardly showing above the ground. These we carried home with her, to open in a dish of moss in the warmth of her sitting-room. And on Ascension Day, which then always began at Wilton with a Communion Service at five in the morning, Miss Sargent was in Grovely soon after six, picking great bundles of bluebells and bracken. She had too that gift of arranging flowers in the peculiarly intimate way which is only possessed by those who love them very much. Miss Sargent was enthusiastic in all things. She was keenly interested in needlework, embroidery and knitting, and was for ever trying some fresh pattern or design. She loved music, books, life—everything— except Mr. Corby. His wife had a long distressing illness, and then Miss Sargent was the best of neighbours, waiting on the invalid, cooking for her, running in to visit her, cheering her with her stores of gossip; but only when the master of the house was out of it. She would not meet him.

Mrs. Corby died during the school holidays, and that week Miss Sargent wrote resigning her post as schoolmistress. She did not even come back to pack her things, but sent a sister to do this for her. A year later, she returned as Mrs. Corby.

This was the explanation. When Miss Sargent first came to Wilton, she had found her neighbour a widower, for Mr. Corby's odd difficult personality secured for him in all three charming wives. He soon asked Miss Sargent to marry him, and was accepted. Before the engagement was announced, the lovers quarrelled bitterly, and then parted for the holidays. Before the next term began, Mr. Corby avenged himself by marrying someone else. So these two lovers became enemies, and lived worlds apart, though side by side. He was a reserved man. She appeared to be a completely openhearted woman. No one can guess at their inner feelings during those years, but they proved themselves to be people of a fine sense of honour, and of great selfcontrol. They might have made a mess of things, but they accepted the consequences without involving other people. During those years they ceased to know each other socially. Mr. Corby made a success of his marriage, and Miss Sargent of her school.

Sinca, 'the Russian Sailor', was a great person in the old Wilton days. Lord Pembroke found him somewhere on his travels, and brought him to Wilton as house-carpenter. He was obviously a Slav, with his short square figure, and his flat face marked with smallpox. He spoke very quickly, in a deep hollow voice, which sounded as if he had his head in a bucket. He never walked, but he ran everywhere, on the level, or up and down the ladders which seemed to be his native place. The Wilton Mummers had a phrase, 'a foreign-off man', and this describes Sinca, who was always 'off' somewhere with his foreignness. Making and letting off fireworks were among his far-fetched tricks, and when we had a display, he was in his element. Then the amazing little figure could be seen, darting in and out of the darkness, now bending behind some curious contraption on a frame, which then fizzled and sparkled, and turned into a whirring Catherine Wheel; now appearing in a completely different part of the scene from which would soon rise the long swoop and the soft explosion of a rocket in the air, its stars falling quietly above a crowd of upturned faces; and then Sinca would be found crouching behind a bouquet of Roman Candles, sending their heart-shaped flowers soaring to the sky. Crackers were child's-play to Sinca, and he loved to set them hopping and sputtering among a crowd of people; for he himself was not unlike a cracker, mischievous and erratic.

Sinca's history was mysterious and romantic. A day or two before the bombardment of Sebastopol, two little Russian boys, aged about four or five, strayed out of the town into the English lines. The soldiers made friends with them, and the General decreed that they should be detained in camp till after the bombardment, as they would be safer behind, than in front of, the British guns. The children were brought into the town with the army, and criers were sent out, asking for their parents. No one claimed them. Their relations were either dead, or had left the town. What was to be done with the little Russian waifs? Two English officers adopted them, brought them home, and had them educated and taught trades. The children could never tell their surnames, and the soldiers named them Alma and

Inkerman. Simeon Sinca was the little boy's way of pronouncing his name of Simeon Inkerman, and so he was called to the end of his life. Thus the Russian sailor came to port at Wilton, where he married the nurse of my elder brothers, and between them they produced a family extremely unlike the Wiltshire children among whom they played.

Albert Musselwhite was the grave-digger, and with his mixture of fun and sentiment, he would have been in his element in the graveyard of Elsinore. Children loved him. He rollicked with them, and had them always under control. I have seen three hundred children screaming with laughter at his jokes at a Band of Hope meeting; and when the noise went beyond bearing, he said: 'See my 'and. When it goes up—SILENCE.' Up went his hand, and you could hear a pin drop.

Generations of children learnt from Albert to be useful, for he knew that no game is so delightful to a child as is being given something real to do. Under his guidance we first learnt to decorate the church, and to arrange the books in the pews, while his own children were adept dusters from the age of three. He was our chief friend from his middle age, when I first remember him, till he had become a very old man with thick white hair and beard.

The church tower was Albert's kingdom. He sat in the belfry, chiming three bells at once, one with each hand and one with his foot, and he taught us to chime them too. On great days, when bonfires were lit on the hills, Albert led us up the long difficult dusty ladders to the top of the tower, whence we looked triumphantly over miles of the country round. My younger sister Mildred was afraid to climb those ladders, but her faith in Albert was so complete that she fearlessly made the perilous journey up and down, perched on his shoulders.

If the church tower was Albert's domain, there were days in the year which were his days. Boat-race day was one. We were hotly on the side of Oxford, so he always teased us by wearing a piece of pale-blue ribbon, and by sending us envelopes addressed in a feigned writing, and containing pale-blue bows inscribed: '*Sure to win.*' But Christmas Day was his chief day in the year, and Albert's Christmas began at least six weeks before December 25th.

About the middle of November, we could never meet Albert without his rummaging in his pocket for a bit of mistletoe, and then began a frantic chase, over house and garden, till the only safety was to lock one's self into the smallest room to be found. There was no sentiment about this. It was a pitched battle, and I have never since experienced so utter a sense of defeat as on those occasions when Albert did catch me and kiss me under the mistletoe. Once he even approached my very dignified mother with two little leaves and a white berry, and we marvelled as we saw that she did not run away, but remained gravely sitting in her chair, and said: 'ALBERT.' This did intimidate him, and he withdrew to chase the boys.

Wilton then had its poet, Edward Slow, the carriage-builder, a man of rugged face and figure, and with a loud resonant voice which sounded all down the street when he met a friend for a quiet talk. He was a master of the old Wiltshire speech, and his rhymes were not merely written in the dialect, but they came up directly from the dialect mind. He was an entirely descriptive writer, and he described what fell under his own eyes. Slow was no visionary. He was a racy and realistic observer, and his subjects were those things which outstand in the memory of the untravelled countrymen—public dinners, foxhunting, or a visit to London. When country fairs are things of the past, Slow's *Our girt Zeptember Vair* will bring before the mind of future generations, exact and living pictures of the events of every hour in the day of the chief West of England sheep fair in the nineteenth century. But by then, the poem will be written in a dead language, for Slow's was the true Wiltshire dialect, unspoilt by any school-board varnish. He was the last of the old minstrels, for his rhymes really came to life when he read or recited them himself, giving immense delight both to himself and his hearers.

Slow had the countryman's distrust of the foreigner, and some few years before the Great War, he received a letter from a German Philological Society, inviting him to go to London to have gramophone records made from his reading of some of his poems, in order to help these scholars to learn the true pronunciation. Slow was immediately suspicious. He was convinced that the Germans had some ulterior motive, and he refused to answer the letter. Several more came, and at last he silenced these determined correspondents with a postcard on which he wrote in his large deliberate handwriting:

'Mr. Slow does not intend to go to London.'

Years afterwards, he read in the *Daily Mail* that the Italian repulse by the Germans had been prepared for by a previous penetration of the villages behind the lines by Germans who had learnt the North Italian patois from gramophone records. He cut this report out of the paper, and carried it for months in his pocket, to show to every one he met, how far-sighted he had been.

Slow believed in a Freemasonry among poets, and thought that they should always be ready to exchange their works one with another. He wrote to Lord Tennyson telling him this, and enclosing a copy of his 'Wiltshire Rhymes', and he was very proud when a copy of the Poet Laureate's poems came in return; and in the train he could always find out when a fellow passenger was a writer, and would get into conversation and arrange an exchange of 'Works'.

Slow's Wilton patriotism was his strongest emotion. His 'Wilton Chronology' contained every important Wilton date from the earliest Saxon records to the last conversazione given by the Mayor in the town hall. Red-letter days in his life were the dates of the bestowal of the 'ancient Borough's' new Charter, or the opening of the new cemetery. Those events excited his deepest emotions. Cemeteries were always favourite spots for Slow, who said that when he visited a new place, his first walk was always to its cemetery. He liked to learn the names on the gravestones.

When his carriage-building days were over, Slow retired to a villa he had built for himself and had called

'Ellandune', which he believed to be the original name of Wilton. Here he collected and read books on local history; and on Wednesdays he repaired to Wilton House to act as guide to visitors. Slow had no æsthetic sensibility, but he knew about the pictures because they had been collected by Earls of Pembroke, and were among the prides of 'our little Borough'. Though the visitors must have been puzzled by his idiom, the personality of their guide would make them realise that at Wilton they were in the heart of the Wessex of King Alfred.

XII

⋆ OXFORD ⋆

It was a surprise to me to find myself at Oxford as a
student of St. Hugh's Hall. My 'home-keeping youth'
had not till then seemed to tend in any such direction.
Only episcopal pressure could have landed me on this
unexpected shore. The present Archbishop of Canter-
bury gave the first gentle impetus. He was not then
even a bishop, but as Mr. Lang, he once gave some
University Extension Lectures on History at Salisbury,
and I went to them with my governess Miss Hocker.
These were followed by the one really proud moment
in my life. After the lectures, there was an examination,
and Miss Hocker and I both entered for it. Only two
names appeared in the first class—hers and mine. Then
Mr. Lang said that I ought to read for History Honours
at Oxford. Thus the seed was planted, but it lay dor-
mant for some years more. Then Bishop Wordsworth
stepped in. In memory of his first wife, he endowed a
scholarship to be held at one of the Oxford Women's
Colleges, and he put pressure on my father to allow
me to enter for it the first time it was awarded. Papa
consented, being convinced that I had no chance of

winning it. So was I. But I unexpectedly did. Then there was the circumstance that the Head of St. Hugh's was Miss Moberly, a cousin of my mother's, and the daughter of yet another Bishop of Salisbury. Though now a 'Scholar', I had not passed Smalls, or any equivalent entrance examination. I knew no Euclid or Algebra, and my only Latin had been taught me by my mother, who knew enough to get my brothers into their private schools. I quickly had some lessons in mathematics from an old schoolmaster in Salisbury and I rubbed up my Latin; but I had to take my University entrance examination at the end of my first term at St. Hugh's. Thus unprepared, I embarked on a University career.

Only one of my fellow-students had, like myself, been educated at home. She was a Scotch girl, and she took to me from the first because she found that I knew how to pronounce the name 'Menzies'. This was my only social success in that first term, and with most of the students I was not popular.

The women's colleges of those days must have been rather like the upper forms in girls' schools, and they had the same laws of etiquette. Of these I was not only ignorant, but I was unaware that they even existed. I went to Oxford thinking that college life was merely a rather cabined edition of ordinary social life, and I blundered badly, not knowing that I was blundering at all. On one occasion, I should have known better, and perhaps I did.

A week or two after I arrived, the Hall gave a party to the students of Lady Margaret Hall next door. The entertainment was to be an extemporized play with rather a large company, and when we met to rehearse it, I found myself in my element. I was used to acting, so I took charge of the rehearsal, planned the scenes, allotted the parts, and told everybody what to do. I was quite unaware of the fact that I had taken too much upon myself, and that the other performers saw that I needed a lesson. Everything seemed to me to be going very well, and then came the night of the party. The guests arrived, and I went to the dressing-room. It was oddly empty. Then there began to arrive messages from one after another of the company saying that they were unable to act. We were reduced to four. They were Florence Etlinger, a gifted creature, half German, half Russian, who afterwards founded an Operatic and Dramatic School in London, and died as she was on the verge of making it a success; Dorothy Words-worth, a great-grand-niece of the poet, who also died young, as she was about to make her début as a Shakespearian actress; Evelyn Hatch, who with her sister Beatrice later made a small success in playing in private houses scenes from 'Jane Austen', 'George Eliot', and 'Mrs. Gaskel'; and myself. We faced each other, listening to the gay chatter of the assembled and expectant audience.

Then I had a good idea. We took our dilemma on to the stage, and called it 'The Sorrows of a Stage-Manager'. I entered alone, hopefully, and then our three performers came on to the stage again and again, bringing the most absurd and ridiculous excuses from the absent ones. With every defection, I recklessly told the few who remained to double, treble, and quadruple their parts.

We made the most grotesque and impossible doubles. The bride 'played opposite' to herself as bridegroom: the victim was her own executioner, and cut off her own head: the subject of a robbery picked her own pocket. The actresses became contortionists, twisting themselves about to be in two places on the stage at one time. We enjoyed it immensely, and so did the audience, who had no idea that anything else had been contemplated. But it was not a tactful thing to do in face of those who should have been behind the scenes.

Fortunately, after this I was ill for some weeks, and before I was able to return to the world of St. Hugh's, Miss Moberly told me with a lurking smile that she had heard of my lack of good college manners. I had talked to my seniors, lounging in a chair with my hands clasped behind my head, and I had even been heard to whistle in one of the passages. This last crime showed great acuteness of hearing on somebody's part, for my whistle has always been fainter than a grasshopper's chirp. Miss Moberly said I must conform to the customs of the college.

In those days, the education of schoolgirls was mainly in the hands of people who believed in the segregation of spinsters. Many schoolmistresses had seldom spoken to a man unless he stood to her in the relation of father, pastor, or tutor. Born a spinster, she had found herself at school with other little spinsters, being taught by more spinsters a few years older than themselves. At those early women's colleges, she met other spinsters from schools like her own. Having passed her university examinations, she hastened back to school to become a teacher in her turn. Her evenings were spent in the Common Room with her fellow-teachers, and her holidays with them, climbing the Alps. In the eyes of the young men of her class, she had always seemed too learned to be spoken to, so there could be for her no escape from this vicious circle. Not of course literally a vicious one, for this mode of life produced more vacuums than vices; and it might indeed be said that the vacuums of yesterday are filled with the vices of to-day.

The life lived by Women University Students was a great surprise to me, as my ideas of a women's college were derived from Tennyson's 'Princess'. Here was no 'Rosebud garden of girls'. Instead I found a lot of young women who seemed to look upon their Oxford years as merely the prelude to a troublesome examination, which would in its turn be the prelude to the life of a schoolmistress.

At St. Hugh's I made acquaintance with what I called the *Femme Servante*, a genus produced where two or three are gathered together, and those two or three are girls. The *Femme Servante* is what her name suggests. When she takes a fancy to another girl (and it is her characteristic to do this very often), her happiness lies in becoming the slave of her friend. St. Hugh's was a poor college with an inadequate staff of servants, and the students had to do a good deal of domestic work for themselves. It was, therefore, a great convenience to find amateurs who were willing to keep fires in,

fill hot-water bottles, make toast, boil kettles, run
errands, brush clothes, wash gloves, or darn vests. I
soon possessed several of these invaluable little creatures, and as I generally saw them doing these very
dull things, the impulse was, not primarily to feel grati-
tude, but to connect them in the mind with all those
things which one most disliked doing for oneself.

In *A Room of One's Own*, Virginia Woolf remarks on
the austerity of life in a women's college compared
with those inhabited by men. This was certainly exem-
plified at St. Hugh's in my day. No one had two rooms,
not even the Vice-Principal, and there were even one
or two double rooms shared by two students. But the
general rule was that everyone had a 'Bed-Sitter', the
bed disguised as a sofa in the day, and often sat upon
in the evening by half a dozen of the guests at one of
the rather tepid 'Cocoas' which took for us the place
of the wines of our 'fast' brothers. Food in college was
plain and boring—mostly very large cods, and legs of
mutton, washed down by water. As the term went on,
however, and faces grew pale and nerves jumpy, there
appeared all down the table, bottles of Burgundy, each
labelled with its owner's name. These were meant to
stimulate the waning vitality of these strenuous students, for they were one and all extremely strenuous.
Their years at Oxford meant little beyond lectures,
essays, and the Radcliffe Library. There were for us
none of those terrific morning conversations which
echo across the quads in the men's colleges, completely
preventing reading except in vacation, but which really
constitute most of the fun of being at once young and

intelligent. At St. Hugh's, everyone worked conscientiously behind closed doors, and the passages were as silent as the catacombs except in those few minutes when the whole college was speeding to eat in Hall or to pray in Chapel. At half-past ten at night, there was generally another outburst. Punctual to the moment, a bell was heard in the passages, and then here and there a door broke open, and there reeled out the besotted guests who had been solidly drinking cocoa inside, since the clock had struck ten half an hour before. For the discipline was supreme, and those parties were timed to the half-minute. No one expected to live her own life, or to keep her own hours. Women's colleges had then an untarnished schoolgirl complexion.

The authorities constantly reminded us that we were not members of the university, but its guests. No university tutor need accept us as pupils. Those who taught us did so from their belief in the Higher Education of Women, and if our manners did not reach the standard they expected from us, they might at any moment refuse to teach us at all. It was like walking the tightrope, for we had to keep a balance between two yawning gulfs. Some tutors boycotted the women's colleges because of the students' lack of charm. One critical don succeeded in stopping hockey for several terms after he once met the teams coming home, and saw the hot and swollen faces of some of his pupils. On the other hand, there were those who disapproved of us for fear that the 'sweet girl graduates' might endanger the morals of the university. I was once reported to Miss Moberly as having worn an amber necklace at a

At Oxford too I knew some remarkable people. First among these was Miss Moberly herself. As I have said, she was a distant relation of my mother's, but my parents had seen little of her since she went to Oxford, and I should never have known her but for St. Hugh's. In her sitting-room there, two family portraits were hung—those of her mother, and of her Moberly grandmother. Miss Moberly's mother, painted by Sir David Wilkie, was a vision of femininity—swan neck, sloping shoulders, oval face, sidelong glance, vast feathered hat with veils, and a little hand fastening a glove. The grandmother had a square dark Slavonic face, and looked from the wall into the room with rather a forbidding expression.

Beneath the portraits of her two very opposite-looking ancestresses, Miss Moberly sat, reading, writing, or playing the piano, and looking up to greet a visitor with a sudden very brilliant smile. She had a fascinating, mellow voice, with an amusing crack in it. Her colour and the contour of her face resembled those of the stern grandmother, but the welcoming smile must have come from the lovely mother. Miss Moberly had been born with a prejudiced and extremely biased nature, but she had told herself that the head of a college should possess wisdom and impartiality, so she made herself develop those qualities. But the old Adam would sometimes peep irresistibly out. As a young woman, she had not been particularly interested in the higher education of women as a cause to be fought for; but she had quite naturally studied Hebrew and Greek, because she couldn't see how anyone could care about the Bible, without wishing to read it in the original languages.

Miss Moberly had then the independent attitude towards learning which is possessed by the natural scholar who has chosen for himself the intellectual pastures in which he will browse; yet she was well aware of the meaning of scholastic discipline. Her father had been Head Master of Winchester, and his years there must have made a considerable impress on his character. He bequeathed to all his family a touch of the schoolmaster. Miss Moberly had it, and she seemed at once to be a decisive head, and a docile subordinate. She ruled her own college, but she was all the time rather frightened of Miss Wordsworth, of a body which sounded to me like the 'Heptagonal Council', and of the kind and pernickety dons who had accepted us as pupils. She constantly warned us of the pitfalls surrounding our paths, as we trod delicately on the stepping-stones she laid down to guide us among the fads and prejudices of these fastidious autocrats.

Miss Moberly alone made St. Hugh's worth while. She was a very exciting head of a college. Music had been her first love, and at St. Hugh's she liked nothing better than to collect a string band or a chorus from among the students, and to work away at some rather difficult music. She was a very good conductor, and also never minded the drudgery of teaching. Unforgettable too are her Sunday evening lectures on the 'Book of the Revelation'. She had high spiritual insight, and she also was saturated with Hebrew symbolism, and knew a good deal of medieval history. All of this was blended in those lectures.

At St. Hugh's I gained Miss Moberly as a friend to the end of her life, and she allowed me to write the introduction to the final edition of 'An Adventure', the little book in which she related her amazing experience at the Trianon. It was this 'adventure' which made her known to a far wider circle than would otherwise have heard of her; and, oddly enough, for years she objected to the subject's being mentioned in her presence. The clairvoyante and the schoolmaster in her did not agree, and she disliked 'spiritualistic' experiences. The book for years had a sort of pseudo-anonymity, and was talked of as the 'Ghost Story of those two Governesses'— which—for anyone who knew her—did not suggest Miss Moberly at all. When she at last consented to admit that she had been the writer, she was unexpectedly pleased with the renewed appreciation which the book received now it was learnt that its writer was so responsible a person.

When I was at Oxford, Lewis Carroll was still living in the rooms in Tom Quad which he had occupied when my father was at Christ Church. He sometimes invited me to dinner. His position in Oxford was such that in his case alone, our rigid rule of chaperonage was waived. If our authorities were sticklers for chaperons, he was equally a stickler for none.

'I only like a *tête-à-tête* dinner,' he said. 'And if you don't come alone, you shan't come at all.'

Miss Moberly gave in, saying with her gay smile: 'Once more, we must make a virtue of necessity.'

Mr. Dodgson (Lewis Carroll's real name) had instituted a fixed technique for his dinner parties. Dinner

[176]

was at seven, and at half-past six, he always appeared at St. Hugh's to walk with me to Christ Church. The walk took exactly half an hour, and at the end of the evening, my host timed our return to St. Hugh's to synchronize with the ringing of the ten-thirty bell in the passages. He left me at the door precisely at that moment, to show his sincere respect for college rules so long as he approved of what they laid down. He used to say that those walks were the best part of his dinner parties. The food was always the same. Only two courses—first, some very well-cooked mutton chops, and then, meringues. A glass or two of port followed, and, an hour after dinner, we had tea. Mr. Dodgson never spoke of Alice in Wonderland; but there were three other things in his life of which he seemed really proud. He spoke of them every time we had dinner together. They were his kettle, his logic, and his photographs.

At eight-forty-five in the evening, he always set about boiling the water for our tea, and Lewis Carroll was very like other old people, in that the same thing always reminded him of the same story. He now told the story of his invention. It appeared that he had noticed that most people either burnt their hands on kettles, or used kettle-holders, which were always dirty, and often lost. He had got a blacksmith to attach to his own kettle a long handle like that on a saucepan, and with this he always lifted his kettle off the fire, and filled the teapot. He boasted about this in a most ingenuous manner. Then he was always in the middle of an argument with the university Professor of Logic, and each time I

[177]

dined in his rooms, he had ready a newly invented
problem of his own, which I was asked to solve 'by
common sense'. My wild guesses were nearly always
lucky enough to agree with Mr. Dodgson's own solu-
tions, and to disagree with those of the Professor; so
we were both very happy, and congratulated each other
a lot. But best of all were his photographs, taken by
him in the days before dry plates were invented. The
wet plate gives great quality to the prints. Mr. Dodgson's were deep, soft, and beautiful. They were mostly
portraits in 'carte-de-visite' size, and very unpretentious, but I have seen no photographs which produce
so delicately the modelling of the face. They were quite
unlike any photographs of to-day, both in this fine por-
traiture, and in the unaffected realism of their setting.
His sitters sat on their chairs and sofas, and round their
own tables, conversing in their tall hats and crinolines,
and seemingly quite unaware that they were posing for
their 'likenesses'. Mr. Dodgson was prouder of his sitters than of his art. He had many portraits of King
Edward VII as an undergraduate, lots of 'Alice' and
the rest of Dean Liddell's family; and there were pages
of Rossettis and Terrys, which I always remember.

Mr. Dodgson was very fond of little girls, and especially of child actresses, or children who loved plays. At
a matinee in Brighton, he once sat in the stalls beside
a little girl of about four, and their mutual enjoyment
made them quickly friends. After the theatre, he tracked
her to her home, and then found out who lived in the
house. Though, as I have said, he never appeared very
proud of having written *Alice in Wonderland*, he quite

appreciated the value of being the author of that book, when he wanted to make a fresh 'child friend'. He now wrote to the mother of this little girl, saying who he was, and inviting the child to tea. He received a curt and crushing reply. The lady wrote:

'The young lady whom you speak of as my "little girl" is not so very childish after all, and she is not my daughter, but my niece. If she were my own child, I should certainly ask you your intentions before allowing her to accept your invitation, and I must do the same now.'

Mr. Dodgson replied that his intentions were honourable, 'though one does not usually have specific "intentions" with regard to a child of four or five.'

By some mistake, the letter had reached the wrong lady, and one who, oddly enough, had been at the same matinee with a niece of nineteen. The episode hurt Mr. Dodgson's feelings very much, and he told me that he thought the name of Lewis Carroll might have been allowed to guarantee the safety of a young girl of any age whatever.

And the real little friend of the theatre never knew what a distinguished conquest she had made that afternoon. If any lady who was a child in Brighton in the 'sixties or 'seventies, may happen to read this book, let her search her memory for a swift and intimate friendship which began and ended one afternoon in the theatre there. She captivated Lewis Carroll.

PREAMBLE

★ SALISBURY CLOSE AND FITZ HOUSE ★

*M*ary *Kingsley found a tribe in West Africa who believed that, when a man has to leave one home for another, his frightened soul escapes from his body and runs away into the wilds. Once there, he will never find it again. But now every man in the tribe has learnt how to lift the fluttering homesick thing very carefully out of his breast before he begins to pack his other treasures. He puts it into a safe box which he gives into the keeping of the priest till he is settled in his new home. Then he goes to collect his lost soul and to bring it back with him.*

I had not read this when we left Wilton, and when we were first living in The Close, I felt very unhappy and forlorn. I wandered about, looking for something, I knew not what; but it was something which I could not find. As the months went on, the cathedral gave me some sort of a substitute for the soul I had lost; and at the time I did not guess what was happening to me. I had then a sort of life, but it never seemed quite like my own; and the nine years which we spent away from Wilton would have left a complete blank in my memory but for the diary which I continued to keep. When at last we came back to The Daye House, I found my lost soul in the park. It had been there all the time; and now it walked back into me of its own accord, and I was myself again.

We left Wilton because my father was too old to go on with his parish work, so for the last seven years of his life, he lived in that house on the north side of The Close which is ear-marked for the senior prebendary, and he took his part in the cathedral services.

The people in The Close were then (and doubtless still are) greatly influenced by their houses. No one living in these can ever be quite commonplace. Very few of our neighbours went to bed without first looking through their windows out into the moonlight or the starlight, to find against the sky the outline of the cathedral, standing apart upon its great sweep of lawn—a silent beatitude. Month by month they watched the stars in their courses journeying in their gigantic wheels over the spire. On summer evenings, the groups which stood gossiping in The Close over the little events of the day, were never altogether oblivious of the beauty of the glowing twilight as it slowly blurred the noble lines and the intricate carvings of the great building.

This subconscious preoccupation with the cathedral charac-terizes most of the natives of Salisbury. At any hour of the day, if a strange bird alights upon the spire, in a very few minutes a shopkeeper or two seems to have felt the impact of his perching. All over the city, men come to their doors and look up. Groups collect, arguing over the breed of the stranger. From this one can judge how lovingly the Salisbury people watch their spire.

Within The Close, the houses cast an almost equal spell upon their owners. And no wonder. There are in England other cathedrals: there is no other Salisbury Close. The whole

*story of English domestic architecture is told within its walls.
The palace is a history in itself. Its park wall was built from
the stones of the Norman cathedral at Old Sarum; and its
vaulted crypt was the hall of the house of that Bishop Poore
who founded the present cathedral in* 1220. *Successive bishops
went on adding to the palace for six hundred years; and during
all those centuries, houses were being built in The Close. There
are the little early ones which were built by Elias the Clerk of
the Works and Robert the Mason, as their own dwellings while
they worked at the cathedral. There is the grand 'King's
House' of the Middle Ages: Bishop Seth Ward's 'Matron's
College' built in the days of Charles II; Wren's 'Choristers'
Schoolroom'; and lastly that triumphant series of elaborate
eighteenth-century houses which represent perhaps the highest
peak ever reached by the builders of town houses in this country.*

*The people who lived in The Close presented a unique com-
bination of elsewhere incompatible attitudes towards their
houses. In the first place, they took them entirely as a matter
of course. There seemed to them nothing remarkable in the
fact that they had been chosen by Divine Decree to run in and
out to their tea-parties through those supremely beautiful
doorways. That—so it seemed to these scholarly canons and
gentle old maids—is what the houses are like in which one
lives. Then there was the other point of view. Their natural
acquiescence in their good fortune never blinded them to the
beauty of their surroundings. No one in The Close was surprised if a passing visitor asked permission to look inside the
door and into the rooms. Such visits seemed as natural as the
milkman's daily call. The lot had fallen unto them in a fair
ground and they knew it; but they were house-conscious rather*

*than house-proud. This peculiar spirit of The Close is diffi-
cult to describe, but it is one of the first things which strikes
one on coming to live there.*

*Our house, like several of the others, was of more than one
date. It was mainly a small narrow eighteenth-century house
with, on each floor, only two perfectly proportioned rooms. This
lovely little building had been tacked on to the end of a medieval
cottage and the two combined made the letter L. Some large
rooms had been added to the back of the house in the nineteenth
century, but as these could not be seen from The Close, their
ugliness injured the house less than their convenience improved
it. Our garden extended to the beautiful old Close wall which
was, however, hidden from view by a row of greenhouses. Here
my father was always happy with his roses and orchids.*

*Our time in The Close included the four war years, fol-
lowed by my father's long illness, and then his death. Perhaps
that is why, when I try to remember that house, I think first of
darkness. It was a dark house. We were overshadowed by the
cathedral. We had a magnificent view of it, its whole length
spread out before our windows. But it prevented any direct
light from falling on to my needlework as I sat in the little
white morning-room in the winter, except between the hours of
twelve and two. Life there had always a shadow upon it—the
shadow of the cathedral, of the war, of illness, or of death. . . .*

*When my father died, my sister and I had to leave The
Close. When as children we sometimes drove to parties at
Fonthill, we always passed a most romantic house which I
used to long to have for my own. This was Fitz House in
Teffont, which many people call the prettiest of all the Wiltshire villages. Just beyond the end of its street, a tiny stream
gushes out of the chalk down, to flow the whole length of the*

village in front of the houses, each of which has its own little bridge connecting it with the highway. This water is said to be the purest in Wiltshire: it is very clear, and it tinkles with a silver voice. Fitz House had lately been bought by our friend Lord Bledisloe and he now offered to let it to us. So this house of my childish dreams became the first in which Mildred and I were raised to the dignity of being householders.

Fitz House stands back from the village street, behind a stone wall, which then was lower than it is to-day, so that passers-by had an uninterrupted view of this charming old farm-house. Our wall edged the stream, and among its stones the golden wagtails nested every year. The house makes almost three sides of a square: the main building, a fifteenth-century farm-house, faces the road; a seventeenth-century wing joins it at right angles on one side, facing the long stone barn on the other. The wing had been built as a store, and was first made habitable by Lord Bledisloe when he acquired the house. My bedroom was in this part, a big room with five windows looking in three directions, and as I lay in bed, I could watch the moon pass all round the house, while owls flew over from barn to wing, hooting with lovely melancholy.

We were warned that Fitz House would be damp; and it is true that springs of the famous Teffont water bubble up under every room on the ground floor, and they keep the grass court outside perpetually green. But our two years there were years of drought, so the cool rippling sounds that all day filled the ear were exquisitely refreshing; and in those summers, when we wanted fresh air, we drove to the downs in the evening to dine on the edge of Great Ridge Wood, while we watched the stars come out over the Dorset distance.

Our Teffont gardener was Cull, a man from the neighbour-

ing village of Chilmark, where the quarries have been worked since the days of the Romans. He was therefore as handy with stones as he was with flowers, so he laid out a pretty little paved garden of Mildred's designing and she planted her roses in its beds. Our garden was small—only the paved piece, with beside it a tiny mountain on which wild cherries grew, the kitchen garden behind the house, and the grass court in front. The fields came so near to the house that we could almost lean out of the windows to pick blackberries and mushrooms, primroses and cowslips.

At Fitz House we first learnt what it meant to have a house full of children; for Mildred and I had come at the end of the Wilton family, looking on our brothers as rather grand young men, who came home from school or from Oxford for the holidays, and who played games which were too serious for us to share. Now there were three families of nephews and nieces; and if Salisbury memories are chiefly memories of shadows, those of Teffont are full of noise and laughter and children's games. All this fun was inspired and led by Mildred, now the perfect aunt as she had ever been the perfect sister.

We lived in Fitz House for two years.

XIII

⋆ FLOODS ⋆

One morning we looked out from our windows in
the Close to see the walls of the Cathedral rising out of
the waters of a great lake, which covered the whole
of the lawn. The effect was magical. The level grass in
Salisbury Close has a far-famed beauty, but this was
like something seen in a dream, or read of in a poem.
No cathedral built of solid stone could be thus isolated: this must be 'La Cathédrale Engloutie' rising
from the waters.

It was the month of January 1915, and the unceasing
rain of that first autumn of the war had turned the five
chalk streams which meet at Salisbury into five raging
torrents which no hatches could control. At the same
time, an exceptionally high spring-tide rushed up the
Avon from the sea. The water could not get away. It
broadened out upon the city.

The interior of the cathedral was even more lovely
than the Close outside. All through the night the water
had been silently coming up through the floor, and by
morning the nave was a large still pool, from which the
pillars rose and into which they threw their reflections.

The medieval glass in the west window made a tangled pattern of light and colour in the water. The nave was quickly emptied of chairs and nothing broke the beauty of its proportions.

The water did not reach the choir, and services were held there throughout the flood, the congregations reaching them upon perilous bridges made of planks. There were none of these on that first morning when my father and Dr. Bourne, another very old canon, arrived for the service, having somehow made their way across the Close. These intrepid veterans were not deterred by the sight of that lake of cold-looking water. They were bent for the vestry which lay beyond it and they meant to get there. Each mounted a chair and armed himself with a second, which he planted in the water in front of him. On to this he now stepped, and then swung into position in front of it the chair he had just vacated. By repeating this manœuvre the two fearless canons made stepping-stones for themselves from west to east of the cathedral.

The second day of the flood was the Festival of the Epiphany. At eight o'clock that morning, the Communion was celebrated in the Lady Chapel behind the choir. It was like the scene of a legendary shipwreck. The cathedral was almost in darkness, though here and there a gas jet threw a light which quivered in the water. As we crossed the plank bridges the faint reflections of the pillars swayed a little beneath us. The cathedral looked much larger than usual—empty, dark, and filled with water; and as Bishop Ridgeway came to the altar, the candlelight fell upon him in his shining cope and mitre, with the Pastoral Staff carried before him. He looked like some little elfin being.

For some time after the floods had gone down, the nave was too damp to be used, so it remained empty of chairs. All through that time we revelled in its lovely spaciousness. Miss Townsend, who has lived all her life in the most distinguished of the Close houses, has a memory for beautiful things, which never seems to fail her. She now recalled the days when all the cathedral services were held in the choir, and one Sunday as she watched her niece leading her little girl down the empty nave, she said: 'It reminds me of what I used to see.' One thinks at once of Trollope or of Bishop Moberly, who wrote in his diary that on the afternoon of his first Advent Sunday at Salisbury, there were only 'a few ladies in the boxes, ill-lighted by candles, attending prayers without a sermon'. The following year, in Advent 1870, he recorded that he had preached 'to a very large congregation in the nave lighted for the first time with gas'.

During this flood of 1915, several of the Salisbury streets were flooded and people went about them by boat. Gina Fisher and I decided that it would be a historic feat to be rowed down Fisherton Street, so we set off for the starting-point, each accompanied by a scoffing sister to watch. I blush to say that our hearts failed us at the crucial moment. We found that there was a considerable gap between the last dry spot where it was possible to walk, and the point where the water was deep enough to float a boat. Stout policemen carried the would-be passengers across this no-man's-land—a most ridiculous sight, which all day attracted a large and hilarious crowd. But this was not the worst. The boat itself was so wet and dirty that no one dared to sit down in it. Everyone had to stand, each man clutching at his nearest neighbour when the boat lurched suddenly. An unexpectedly big lurch always sent two or three people into the water, so that the lookers-on had plenty of fun for their money. We watched the scene for some time and then we agreed that although we had been right to think that this would be a historic occasion, yet it was better to watch history in the making than to make it ourselves.

At Wilton people went to their work in farm wagons which plied busily up and down the streets in the early hours, and the curate was pushed to church in a wheelbarrow. One morning, while it was still almost dark, the people in West Street looked out of their windows and saw an unreal and fairy-story figure looming through the twilight. A giant seemed to have risen from the waters and was now making his way from the outskirts of the town. There was no doubt as to his alarming proportions, for his head was level with the upper windows, and when he came nearer it was seen that the water splashed on each side as though Leviathan himself were churning it up. This super-man turned out to be Frank Haines, the Wilton House carpenter, who had got up early to make himself an enormous pair of stilts. As long as the flood lasted he walked on these the mile which separated his house from his work.

All sorts of horse vehicles were pressed into the service of the marooned inhabitants. The Herbert children filled their pony-carriage with stores which they took to the flooded houses and then cords were dropped from the upper windows to fish up the provender. Fred Rawlence then possessed that now-forgotten thing a double dog-cart, and to this he harnessed his old grey horse. He took with him a ladder and many cans of hot soup. His quarry was any old person who was too feeble to get out of bed to fish for himself. Fred drove his dog-cart against the wall of the house he was visiting and planted his ladder on the seat of his dog-cart. Up it he climbed and into the window with his can of soup.

A Canadian Regiment which was stationed near-by sent its ambulance to rescue two old people who were too ill to be left in their flooded house. It was a very difficult feat to get them through the window and down the ladder on stretchers, but this was brilliantly done; and then arose an unexpected complication. The two old things refused to be saved without their cocks and hens which were shivering on a beam in a shed near the house. The gallant Canadians were ready for this rescue too. They waded into the shed, and made grab after grab at the squawking, fluttering, frightened birds, who violently objected to being saved. They made a good fight for it amid the shouts and laughter of the soldiers, who finally captured them all and triumphantly conveyed their clucking captives through the streets to Fred Rawlence's dry chicken-run at Bulbridge.

Such floods never arose entirely without warning. The water-keepers (Drowners as they call them in Wiltshire) controlled the rivers as well as they could,

G

raising and lowering the hatches so as to allow the water to pass through by degrees. Then they sent warnings to the various villages on the banks to say at what hour the flood was likely to reach each place. When these messages came, people who lived in houses near the stream began carrying upstairs the furniture from their lower rooms. Having done this, they generally refused to leave their houses, preferring to remain encamped on their upper floors, for they always hoped that the flood would not be so deep as it had been last time.

Two women lived alone in a cottage standing some way back from the main Wilton Street. They received the customary flood warning and they decided to stay on in their house, as the mother, a very old woman, was ill in bed. The daughter carried upstairs as many of their possessions as she could manage, and she stacked them in a little unused bedroom. They lit a fire in the only other room on the first floor, and there they awaited events. They heard the water rush into the house. It gurgled and swished round the kitchen table. It poured out of the downstairs windows. It began coming up the stairs, and from it an icy draught came under the door into the room where the two women were listening. The old mother grew worse. Bronchitis set in. When it began to grow dark, a policeman waded to their door and asked whether they needed help. They said they only wanted a bottle of medicine from the doctor. This had always made the old woman better before and they were sure it would do so again. The policeman brought it and handed it up. Thus they faced the night.

Miss Turner built up the fire and gave her mother some of the doctor's medicine. They were now completely cut off from human kind. From the window it was possible now and again to see a faint gleam upon the wilderness of black water which heaved round the walls outside; and the chill air mounted relentlessly into the room in spite of the fire which burnt in the grate. An hour or two was enough to kill the old woman. Her breathing became more and more difficult. She struggled—and then she struggled no more. The room became absolutely still, 'but for the unending sound of the water outside and for the occasional fall of a cinder in the grate.

Miss Turner laid a sheet over the face of her dead mother and waited hour after hour for morning. She dared not plunge into the water outside because it was so dark that she could not judge its depth, and there was no house near enough for her to call anyone to help her with the last offices. Thus they stayed till morning —the living woman watching beside the dead.

When dawn began to break, Miss Turner went downstairs into the flooded room. She could not open the door for the weight of water against it, but she managed to get through the window and she plunged into the flood outside. The water was above her waist and it was cruelly cold. Physically, she had hardly the strength to battle with it, but her resolution enabled her to struggle to the nearest house. That 'little mother', of whose delicate beauty she had been so proud, must be decently laid out for the grave, and she had not the skill to do this herself. Each hour that passed would make the task more difficult, so she would not wait till morning had really come before she went for help.

That day it was not possible to bring a coffin to the house, and when night came no persuasion could prevail upon Miss Turner to leave her mother's body there alone. The dead woman lay uncoffined on her bed and her daughter watched beside her. From time to time she made herself a cup of tea, boiling the water on the fire in that one room. Friends fought through the flood to sit with her and to beg her to come away with them. She welcomed their sympathy, but she would not leave the house. Calm with the dignity of love and of grief, she waited alone through the hours; for *'many waters cannot quench love, neither can the floods drown it'*.

XIV

★ WAR ★

When King George V was crowned in 1911, Sidney, my sailor brother, brought a contingent of bluejackets to London for the Coronation. They acted as Guard of Honour to the Archduke Franz Ferdinand of Austria. During that week, Sidney said to one of my other brothers:

'I really ought to kill this man, not to guard him.'

'Why?'

'Because, according to the Great Pyramid, he is going to start the Great War of 1914.'

It seems to me quite impossible reasonably to believe in the prophecies of the Great Pyramid, and yet it is equally impossible for me to deny that Sidney was always right about it. He believed in it implicitly, though he did not always agree with other people's readings of its meaning. He preferred to work out his own calculations from the complicated measurements of those galleries and chambers and tunnels; and he came to very precise conclusions.

In September 1914, when this first prophecy of his had been so direfully fulfilled, and my brother Harold

[197]

had already been killed on the Aisne, I asked Sidney what he could foretell as to the length of the war.

'I can't say exactly,' he said. 'But it won't be over by Christmas as you all imagine. It can't possibly last beyond December 31st, 1918, but the end won't be more than a month or two before that.'

We could not then believe him.

War is now like a wolf at the door, and we for ever hear it growling. It is to-day the world's obsession, and before 1914 it was seldom in the mind of an ordinary person as an actual possibility. The word *war* conjured up pictures of the Battle of Waterloo, of Florence Nightingale, or perhaps of South Africa. We could most of us remember that last war, but it seemed to have been a very hole-and-corner affair, affecting our daily lives very little. It did not seem then so remarkable that Jane Austen should have lived through the Napoleonic Era without so much as mentioning the war in her novels.

Yet Wiltshire was probably looked upon, at the beginning of the twentieth century, as an especially military area. The Southern Command Headquarters was at Salisbury, and there were always troops training on the Plain. When we sat in the garden on hot summer mornings, we often heard the distant boom of big guns. It did not seem a warlike sound. It came associated with gardening and with the scent of flowers; and that long soft sustained rumble was in itself drowsy and peaceful. It belonged to happy summer days.

For most English people living in the first fourteen years of the century, the prospect of war was thus remote and unrealizable. It did not seem a thing which could ever actually enter into our lives. We laughed at my brother Harold for the sulky expression on his face in a newspaper picture which showed him at Tilbury, seeing off the German Emperor after his last visit to England.

Harold said: 'Of course I look sulky. He'll kill me some day.'

This was a joke at the time, but those words came true in the very first month of the war.

Then Henry Newbolt wrote to me.

'This war is going to change the world for us all. Nothing will ever be the same again.'

Once again I could not believe him. In those first months of the war, it seemed that the only people for whom the world must be for ever changed, were those who had lost someone they loved. But this is the least of the effects of the war. 'Pre-war' and 'post-war' are as distinct from each other as are two Geological Periods; and the lost lives which meant so much to us, are, for the new generation, merely like fossils indicating the separate strata of that (to them) pre-historic epoch. The war is now studied in its broad effect on western civilization. What that effect really was it is hard as yet to say; but what strikes me personally, perhaps more than anything else, is that it has made our civilization self-conscious, and vocally self-conscious. Before the war we were quite satisfied that modern progress was taking its course and that all was improving with the world. We did not think overmuch about this and we lived our lives and enjoyed them. But now, from morning to night, we discuss ourselves, our predecessors, and our

possible successors, and most of this discussion is profoundly pessimistic. I think this is a very outstanding
characteristic of to-day as compared with yesterday.

In 1914, we had for two years been living in The
Close. Then, as now, its walls held peace as in a cup.
The great elms had not then been felled; and their
broad shadows lay gently upon the grass which surrounded the cathedral like a flat green pool. Many visitors came in summer; and in the afternoons, nurses
brought children to play upon the grass. The voices of
visitors and of children alike were always subdued by
their consciousness of the beneficent though resolute
presence of the Close constable, who moved about
near by, watching their doings with a disapproval
which was never altogether unfriendly. At night, when
the Close gates had been locked, and the Compline
bell had sounded from the Chapels of the Palace and
of the Theological College, the Close was lulled into
a complete silence. The guests coming home from a
Canon's dinner party always took care to step very
quietly through the Close, much as people, coming late
into their houses, tiptoe past bedroom doors so as not
to awake the sleeping family. For the Close was a family
party. We all knew if people were going out late, and
if we were awake we listened to hear them come home;
but if we were asleep, we were annoyed when they
woke us up. The city outside the Close walls seemed
very far away; and when we sat in the garden on summer nights, my father often remarked that it was almost incredible that twenty thousand people could be
living a few hundred yards away.

On the first Sunday in August 1914, this perpetual peace of the Close was broken by the constant reiteration of the word 'War'. All through the previous week, that ugly word had prowled about outside, like a black panther trying to get in. Staff officers had hurried to and fro looking serious, but the Close took no more interest in Balkan affairs than did the rest of England. Few people even knew the name of the murdered Archduke, and nobody wanted to go to war about him.

Then, on that Sunday, the panther was inside the Close and at our doors. The wild beast had leapt across Europe, and was now, not in the Balkans, but in Belgium. In these after-days, people sometimes speak as if the country had been hurried into war by newspaper propaganda inspired from above; but nothing could be less true. To begin with, propaganda, as we know it to-day, is one of the horrid legacies of the war. As was the case with barbed-wire, in pre-war days people hardly knew what it meant. But, also, the newspapers were taken by surprise. They were busy with Irish affairs. The Government could not dictate a policy to them, for the Government itself was not agreed, and the Cabinet was divided until the very day that war was declared.

The country made up its mind first of all. As a whole it knew little of foreign politics, less about the military strength of the various powers, and least of all about the possibilities of modern warfare. Its first desire was to be let alone. But in some forgotten corner of his memory, every Englishman knew that we had pledged our word to protect the neutrality of Belgium; and up from those forgotten corners there now sprang the consciousness that in honour we must now keep that pledge. We might dread the suffering and the sacrifice of war, but unexpectedly we found ourselves dreading even more the possibility that the Government might fail in what we could not doubt was our duty. On Sunday morning the Press seemed to think that we might keep out, and then young officers on the Plain talked of sending in their papers and of joining the French Army should we fail to keep our word; while my brother Sidney was so disgusted at the suggestion that such a thing could be possible, that he took the Sunday newspapers out into his garden and burnt them on the lawn. The attitude of mind of these days seems largely to have been forgotten, but I find it expressed very clearly in my journal.

On Monday it seemed as if the war was within our very gates. The green shade of the Close was unexpectedly invaded by swarms of dusty, exhausted soldiers. They lay about upon the grass as if they had come from some far-off battlefield and now could go no farther. Who could they be? Rumours fluttered out from every door. And with them there fluttered out too the Canons' wives and the old ladies, all followed by neat maidservants carrying trays of tea to the tired soldiers. Thus the Close reacted to the trumpets of war. With cups of tea.

Our troops proved to be more thirsty for tea than for blood, and more accustomed to it. They were our own local Territorials, youths from the neighbouring villages, on their march to the Plain, where they had been ordered to take the place of regiments leaving for France. They had tramped into Salisbury to learn that their camps were not yet ready for them; and the Dean had found them resting on the pavements in the dusty streets. He at once gave them the freedom of the Close; and there they stayed till night, lying on the grass, singing songs, and enjoying the tea and fruit which was lavished on them from every house. No one then believed that these irregular troops were destined to go overseas. We all thought the war would easily finish without them.

So it began in an uprush of idealism and ignorance. We did not hate the Germans; and when we heard that they were singing a 'Hymn of Hate', directed specially against the English people, we only laughed and said that like other foreigners they had no sense of humour. Like Mrs. Partington with her broom, we faced the World War with cups of tea and a sense of humour. These had hitherto settled most of the emergencies of our generation.

Thus unprepared, undisciplined, and ingenuous, with what patience and endurance did the youth of that day face the miseries of those eternal four years. They were braver than soldiers had ever before been asked to be; for they fought with unseen enemies who showered disease from the sky; they lived for months like moles and rats in dug-outs underground; they died slowly on barbed-wire entanglements amid seas of mud.

In the Close we were very far from these war horrors, yet the war invisibly regulated all our lives. Outwardly, no place changed less. It remained as quiet as before, though the Salisbury streets roared with lorries carrying war material, and were crowded with soldiers from every part of the British Empire. Yet within the Close walls, we still heard only the clock which chimed the hours, various bells tolling as usual for the services, and the floods of music which twice a day gushed out through the open windows of the cathedral. This un-altered peace was the chief gift which Salisbury had to give to the soldiers who passed through the city on their way to and from the Front. All through the war they continued to come through the Close gates to drink in this miracle of celestial quietude. Dean Page Roberts had always considered hospitality to be the first virtue of a Dean, and now he welcomed to the Deanery, the Close and the Cathedral, any who cared to come from among the many thousands of lonely strangers who in those years found themselves stranded in Salisbury.

On Sundays, the cathedral was crowded from the choir to the west doors with soldiers in uniform. At the far end, they could hardly hear one word of the service, for some of the canons had very old and cracked voices, and then the men pulled newspapers from their pockets and read them. But there always came a moment when every one of these was folded up and put away. This was when the Dean began to read the Lesson. He had a magnificent voice and a great sense of rhythm; and all through those years he insisted that no one but he should read these grand passages from the Old Testa-ment. He always used the Authorized Version although there was a copy of the Revised Version provided on the lectern; and every man in the farthest corner of the cathedral seemed to listen spellbound while that fine voice rolled forth the glorious poetry which the Dean loved so much himself.

On Sunday evenings, he instituted a 'Popular Service' in the cathedral for the benefit of this huge passing population. He did not wish to call upon the cathedral choir for this extra service, so he asked me to collect an amateur choir to lead the singing. We only had to sing a very few notes before the whole congregation took up the tune and carried it along at its own pace. Our little choir was placed on two rows of chairs facing north and south at the top of the nave. On the first Sunday, when the service was over, the Dean stopped when he reached our seats on his way to the vestry, and he very ceremoniously bowed to me. For a moment I did not know how to take this; but then I dropped a low curtsey, and the other women bobbed too, while the men solemnly bowed from the waist. After this, we went through this little ceremony every Sunday night, and the Colonials believed it was a quaint old Salisbury custom.

All the big Wiltshire houses—Wilton, Longford, Longleat—were soon turned into hospitals and nearly all the girls became V.A.D.s. Lady Bath told me a very strange story about the Longleat hospital. She had been an invalid for years, and had to be nearly always on her back; but she generally got off her sofa and joined the family when they were about half-way through dinner, making her way alone through the house and leaning on her two sticks. One evening, a year or two before the war, she came out of her sitting-room alone and was about to pass through the hall, where the great staircase was very dimly lit, for there was then no electric light at Longleat. As she approached she saw to her horror that the staircase seemed to be enveloped in smoke and that many people were escaping obviously from a fire. Men were stumbling down the stairs, wearing a light blue uniform which was quite unknown to her. Stretcher bearers seemed to be carrying out dead bodies. Vivid as this scene was, Lady Bath also realized at once that it was unreal and she stepped back and watched it till it faded out. That night she told her daughter what she had seen, and three years later the dreamlike episode actually took place exactly as she had seen it. Longleat was by then being used as a hospital and the patients wore the blue uniforms which Lady Bath had foreseen, but which, at the time she saw it, had not been designed. A fire broke out in the house and the patients hastily escaped down the staircase, and Lady Bath saw, once more, the stretcher bearers of her dream carrying out the men who were too ill to walk.

By the way, Longleat is the only house in which I ever slept with the words '*Out of Bounds*' inscribed above my bedroom door. Practically the whole house had been given over to the hospital, leaving very few rooms for the family and their guests; and these private rooms, which were scattered about in different parts of the house, were all thus distinguished.

During the first year of the war, the resources of the country were organized under a hybrid system which was partly voluntary and partly compulsory. In the long run the compulsory method (which, with spiteful affection was named D.O.R.A.) was destined to win, though nothing could have been more alien to the spirit of this country. By degrees our whole mode of life was changed. In the first three days after war was declared, the banks were closed all over the country, to give time for the hasty printing of £1 and 10s. notes. On August 8th, we saw in Salisbury for the first time that paper currency with which the present generation has grown up. Till then I had looked with some scorn upon the dirty little notes for small sums which were circulated in foreign countries; but when they were introduced here, we accepted them as one of the unpleasant things which, as patriots, we were bound to endure in our country's time of stress. We did not then believe that sovereigns and half-sovereigns were gone for ever. Prices went up, though not startlingly; and at first the slight difference in the cost of things acted as a kind of automatic rationing. One was obliged to buy less, in order to keep the books near their previous level. Till then our tradesmen had always called for orders, which were given to them by the cook at the door; but now I decided to go myself to the market and shops to see what was obtainable every day and at what cost. I found that I saved about £4 a month by this system and I rather enjoyed it. It made keeping house far more amusing for the housekeeper, whatever the unhappy members of the household may have thought about it. The papers were full of economy hints, and we were taught to make marmalade from carrots, butter from potatoes, and cabbage from rhubarb leaves. This last proved to

[207]

be a particularly deadly poison, and it was generally discontinued after a few deaths had been definitely traced to this charming little economy.

One economy which I personally enjoyed very much was bread-making. As soon as bread was rationed, we found that we were allowed the same weight per head of bread or of flour and could draw our ration in whichever we chose. I decided that I would make all the bread which should be eaten in our house. Before I began, I went to consult Mr. Bowle, the Salisbury miller, about the various kinds of flour. He told me such wonderful things about his trade that it seemed that anyone who could not be a poet should certainly be a miller. There must always be something magical in living in a mill house over the millrace with the mill-wheel turning day and night; but there is more romance than that to be found in a mill. The grain itself is full of character. It goes on living after it has been harvested, and it does not even die when it has been crushed between the millstones. It for ever continues to feel changes of climate and to show changes of temper. Mr. Bowle said that the flour would always vary with the course of the stars under which it was milled. Having learnt thus that flour is erratic enough to excuse any faults of the breadmaker, I started on my new career and baked three times a week, using a great variety of different recipes. My bread was quite delicious and I was not the only person who thought so. I soon found that the only secret of bread-making is sufficient kneading, and I pummelled away for nearly an hour each time, always learning a Sonnet of Shakespeare as I worked. By the end of the war I knew them all, but now I can't remember one. I once asked Pamela Grey how she and Lord Grey succeeded in keeping in mind the great quantity of poetry which they could always say by heart. She said that they took much trouble about it, constantly reciting poetry to each other, when they were travelling by motor or in the train, or wherever they found a free half-hour.

When we were at Weymouth in August 1915, we steamed round the harbour and saw the hull of the old battleship, *Hood*, which had been partly sunk at the entrance to Portland Harbour to act as a defence against submarines. She was lying keel uppermost and was a most wonderful colour, burnished yellow and gold. The sailors at Weymouth were then discussing all possible reasons for the sinking of the *Lusitania*. She seemed to have been very far from her prescribed zigzag course, and if she had kept to it she would have been safe.

It was just at this time that a 'National Register' was instituted. This was a kind of voluntary conscription. Everyone between the ages of fifteen and sixty-five was asked to enrol in it and to say what their usual employment was and what they were willing to do. My father was then eighty-four, but he insisted on enrolling. He knew that there was no chance of his being accepted as a chaplain at the Front and he reluctantly contented himself with volunteering to take the place of a younger clergyman who might be sent there.

XV

* THE WOMEN'S LAND ARMY *

During the summer of 1915, I began to think a great
deal about the farms in Wiltshire. I was already on good
terms with many of the farmers near Salisbury, as for
years I had carried on a branch of the National Poultry
Organization Society. I now felt sure that before long
there would be no able-bodied men left on the farms
and that women would have to carry on their work. I
talked this over with Lady Pembroke, and then we discussed it with Lord Bath, the Chairman of the Wiltshire
County Council. He agreed that the day must come
when women would be needed, but he also knew that
the farmers would hate taking female labourers until
they were actually driven to it. He tactfully advised us
to hold our tongues and to keep ourselves in readiness.
I also had a good deal of talk on the subject with Charles
Bathurst, afterwards Lord Bledisloe. He thought that
the question might become imminent sooner than we
expected, as he then believed that all men of military
age would be called to the Colours directly after the
forthcoming harvest. But it was not until the summer
of 1916 that the County Agricultural Committee first

asked us to begin training girls as milkers. Wiltshire
was thus a pioneer in what eventually developed into
the Women's Land Army. We began on a very small
scale. Mr. Louis Greville lent us a cottage at Woodford
where we installed six would-be milkers with a very
entertaining old Miss Snow as matron of the little hostel. She was the sister of a General and looked like one
herself. The girls were taught to milk by Mr. Greville's
dairyman. Several problems arose in that first August.
There was naughty Florrie, who was thought to be
insane, because she jumped out of the window a night
or two before she was going to her first place. We sent
for the doctor, who found no traces of insanity and so
she went off to Heytesbury but was soon returned as
too unmanageable to stay. Then there was Emma, from
Dorchester—a most alarming creature. She was expected to arrive one morning, and I met train after
train till between eight and nine at night, when she
arrived at Salisbury and flew into a furious passion on
the station because she was not allowed to take her
bicycle to Woodford. She sprang at me like a pale
murderess, and then thought better of it and leapt on
to her bicycle, saying she should ride back at once to
Blandford. I hoped that she would, but as a matter of
fact she changed her mind and rode to Woodford,
where she and the sporting Miss Snow after all got
on very well together. A few days later I found all the
Woodford girls in floods of tears, because somebody
had brought 'things in the head' to the hostel; and after
this I was called on to deal with someone whom I described as 'a tart who stinks of onions'. She soon re-

turned whence she came, as she did not like the dairy-man.

After a few months of this, Lord Radnor offered us the Longford Estate Office, where we had room for twice as many girls as we could take at Woodford. These Longford pupils were girls of the so-called 'educated' classes, and I always met them at Salisbury station and drove them to Longford. The first time I went to meet a batch, I accosted all the most attractive-looking girls that I saw and asked if they were coming to the Dairy School. Most of them looked very much offended, and, drawing themselves up with great haughtiness, they answered: 'No.' I learnt my lesson, and the next time I met a train I asked the girls:

'Are you coming to Longford Castle?'

They always looked rather flattered at this, and if I had made a mistake they answered quite apologetically 'No, not to-day'. Then they watched with impressed faces as I led off my little band.

At this time we made a register of about four thousand women, living in Wiltshire villages, who volunteered to go into the fields at times of seasonal emergency and to work as unskilled labourers. These women were useful in harvesting and weeding, but it was becoming obvious that a far more organized service was essential. In the October of that year I went to a meeting at the House of Commons to discuss creating a National Organization to carry on what had hitherto been done sporadically by County Agricultural Committees. We learnt from the Director-General of recruiting that every available man on the farms would have to be called up by the following April and that our Women's Committees would have to fill the gaps. He said: 'No man is indispensable except in the fighting line.' My cousin Sydney Olivier was then President of the Board of Agriculture, and I had tea with him that day to discuss the various plans. All through the following winter, we held meetings with farmers in different parts of the county to explain what was going to be done. They all hated the idea of this 'Regiment of Women' coming into their farms, and it was a very depressing experience to go from place to place outlining our programme, and to be met everywhere by rows of silent, antagonistic faces.

The new Women's Land Army was a corps of women and girls who enlisted for the duration of the war, were given uniform suited for farm work, and, after a preliminary training in the various branches of agricultural labour, were allotted to farms as they were required.

We recruited the Land Army in co-operation with the Labour Exchanges, and we held our Selection Committees in their offices. One day a candidate appeared who was described on her application form as the daughter of a 'Butler'. She did not give the required two references as to character, saying that she knew no one who could speak for her. I said: 'Surely one of your father's employers would give you a character.' On this she looked very blank and said nothing.

One of the ladies on the committee here whispered to me that I had made a mistake. The girl's father was no 'Butler'. He was a 'Cutler'—a gipsy man who went about the village streets grinding knives on a wheel.

We eventually managed to find out something about the girl, and we took her. She was a wild creature, supremely good at managing horses and cattle, but quite unable to live with other girls in the hostel. She refused to eat in a room with other people, but she would heap her food on a plate and go away alone to eat it outside. She told me strange stories of her life. One winter they found an empty house in a lonely part of the downs, and then a lot of other gipsies joined them and they took possession of it and lived there all through the winter. If anyone was seen approaching, the gipsies cleared out and hid in a wood near-by till the stranger had passed. They lit no lights at night lest these should betray them; and the rooms in the house were dark except on moonlight nights. Sometimes tremendous fights sprang up in the darkness. They often began by a man giving his wife a thrashing. The woman screamed and so did other women. One after another joined in till the brawl became general, everybody hitting out right and left. After a time the floor used to become oddly slippery, and then in the morning they would find it covered with blood.

Now that the Land Army was an official organization, we had to keep a great many fresh rules. We soon had five or six training schools in different parts of the county, and one of my first official jobs was to hold a court martial in one of these, on a girl who one night got out of bed and clambered out of the window. I acted as President of the Court and a Board of Agriculture official came to show us how to conduct the case. I never saw a more hideous monster than the prisoner, and the Prosecuting Officer asked her a question which I thought was a foolish one, as there seemed no likelihood of its being answered. She said:

'What did you go out for?'

The girl would have made her fortune on the stage. She took every advantage of her hideous face, and showed great histrionic skill in pausing for some time before she answered, and turning her head from side to side with the most ridiculously coy expression. This interval attracted all eyes to her face, and then she said with a grin:

'Because two boys wanted to see me again.'

Obviously no boy could ever wish to see her once, much less twice; and I had great difficulty in saving myself from breaking into a *fou rire* which would have ruined my reputation in the Land Army.

One morning I got an S.O.S. message from one of our North Wilts workers asking me to come at once to deal with a most critical case. When I arrived I found that this lady had been away from home for a few days, during which her secretary opened a letter from a farmer's wife complaining that her husband was carrying on a liaison with one of the milkers whom we had sent him. The secretary at once wrote and accused the farmer of seducing the girl and threatened to remove her. The farmer declared that he would prosecute the Land Army for defamation of character and he demanded the name of the informer. The wife implored not to be given away.

I could not think what to do, and could only rely on my very official appearance in stiff khaki uniform, which made me look a great deal more important than I felt. Two members of the Committee came with me and we were shown into the dining-room to wait. As I sat there I prayed earnestly that I might know what to say when the farmer appeared. I looked out of the window and saw him going out of the house and disappearing among the sheds with a gun in his hand, and I sat for some time expecting to hear a report. I did not. After a while he came in, still carrying the gun, and he sat down facing me on the opposite side of the dinner-table, against which he leant the gun. Thus we faced each other—I, flanked by my two lady supporters, and he with his quaking wife on one side, and on the other, the rather impudent-looking girl who had been accused.

I opened the interview by saying in a very dignified tone:

'If you will look at your contract, you will find that the Land Army has the right of moving its members from farm to farm at its own discretion. I propose now to remove Jane Smith from here. I think you probably know my reason, but I advise you not to ask me for it.'

He looked taken aback, and said after a moment:

'Will this do any injury to the girl?'

I told him he could leave that to me.

By this time he looked frightened and he said:

'What am I to do if you take my milkers away? I have seventy cows in milk and only one man to milk them. Will you let me have another girl?'

I answered: 'I will ask your wife what she thinks about that.' Then, turning to the wife, I said: 'Would you like to have another milker?'

She said that she would. Neither the farmer nor the girl had another word to say and I made the exchange the next day. Then Jane Smith came to see me in my office. She told me that she was hopelessly in love and couldn't live without this farmer. I felt very sorry for her, but I had to tell her that I was sure that he had not the slightest intention of leaving his wife and children for her sake. She had come into his life too late and would never mean anything to him. I begged her to make up her mind to forget him; and as, by the rules of the Land Army, I was now obliged to discharge her, I put her into a gang of unenrolled girls who were planting trees in Grovely Forest, and I hoped she would pull herself together and be happy there. After that, she three times ran away from Grovely and went back to the farm, and each time the farmer himself brought her back to me and begged me to keep her. At last I had to send her back to her relations, as there was nothing more I could do for her. I never knew what became of her.

Towards the end of the war, when the shortage of food became very acute, recruiting processions went through the East End of London with speakers and bands collecting recruits for the Women's Land Army from the streets and lanes of the city. These were then sent to the various counties in parties of about twenty or thirty, and we tested them for a fortnight or so before they were actually enrolled. Very few of these women knew anything about country life and many of them were quite unsuitable for farm work. Two of our would-be milkers were terrified at their first sight of a cow, having expected that they would look like the joints of meat hanging in butchers' shops, which had hitherto been their only acquaintance with cattle.

On the day after they arrived, I always had a personal interview with each of the recruits, and one morning there came in rather a pretty little woman who was the wife of a Canadian soldier with whom she had come across. She looked so desperately ill that I said I thought she was not strong enough for farm work. She answered me very politely:

'I am always very pale and I assure you it doesn't mean anything. But Madam, I hope you will pardon me for appearing before you without any make-up. I promise you it shall not occur again. Salisbury seems rather a one-horse place and I wasn't able to find anything this morning.'

I thanked her and accepted her apology.

A few days later the matron of the hostel sent for me to come at once to discharge this Mrs. Harding, who had come in roaring drunk the night before, had been sick all over the bedroom which she shared with two other girls, and was now in a most violent and defiant mood. I knew that my uniform would hide my fears, and I nerved myself to meet this virago.

Mrs. Harding was brought in before me by the matron. She did not look violent at all, but more ill even than she had looked the day she arrived.

I said to her: 'I hear you were the worse for drink last night.'

I expected an outbreak of violence, but instead she

looked quite miserable and said nothing at all. I went on:

'You know I said when you joined that I thought your health was not good enough for this work, and I still think so. Possibly quite a little drink will bowl you over, when other people would not be affected at all. But you now wear the King's uniform, and it would never do for you to be seen drunk in the street, so I am afraid I must give you your railway ticket and send you back to London this afternoon.'

She burst into tears and begged me to hear what she had to say.

She then told me that both her parents had been confirmed drunkards, and that when she was three years old, a philanthropical society had taken her from them and sent her to Canada. She had lived there ever since, and had been so carefully guarded that she had never tasted drink. When she came to London she went to stay with a sister who was still living there. This woman was a drunkard too. In her house Mrs. Harding tasted spirits for the first time, and from that moment she had been quite unable to stop, and had drunk steadily for a fortnight. After this she realized what was happening to her and resolved to pull herself together. She thought that her only hope was to get away from London and to join the Land Army. She ended by saying, 'If I go back to London, I know I shall be dead in less than a month.'

I was much moved by this story, and after a good deal of talk with the woman, I suggested that she should sign a pledge promising to become a teetotaller for as long as she remained in the Land Army. She agreed to accept her discharge without question if and when she broke this pledge. I made the signing of the pledge into something of a ceremony, the matron and I both solemnly witnessing the signature.

The next problem was what was now to be done with Mrs. Harding. She was a skilled milker, who in the ordinary course would swiftly have been drafted off to a dairy farm in some village where she would have been alone in lodgings. I told her this and pointed out that she might feel lonely and depressed entirely among strangers, and that this would make it harder for her to keep sober. The alternative was to send her with a gang made up from girls who were now in the hostel to work for a few weeks at forestry in Grovely. This would mean plenty of company, but I was obliged to tell her that she might not find it very congenial company. Her dormitory companions of the previous night were furious with her and I thought the whole gang might be unfriendly. She put herself most touchingly into my hands. Afterwards I told her story to the other women and asked them if they would do their best to help Mrs. Harding and so really to save her life. They showed the most delightful spirit, promising to do their best to keep her happy and to save her from a relapse. She stayed with that gang for some months and was quite sober all the time. Her husband was, before long, badly wounded and invalided out of the Army, and then she went back to Canada with him. I have often wondered what happened to Mrs. Harding. It was a most tragic instance of the hereditary effect of alcohol.

I have never felt more sorry for anyone, and I greatly admired the way in which the other women rallied round her and helped her along.

One Saturday evening one of our Group Leaders brought in two girls who wanted to join the Land Army that very night, saying that they could give no references as to their character. They were art students, and they looked very superior and refined. When I tried to find the reason for all this hurry and mystery, the Group Leader said:

'May I tell Miss Olivier?'

They said that she might.

She then told me that one these girls had been going to be married on the following Monday, but that her engagement had suddenly been broken off. She had therefore fled from home, and she now wished to bury herself in the heart of the country.

I still maintained that I could not enrol her till Monday, and I told her to come to me alone that morning. When she came I said to her:

'Tell me what happened about your engagement.'

She answered: 'Well you see, I got mixed up with a gang of the greatest jewel thieves in Europe.'

Clutching at my few poor treasures I said:

'Are you a jewel thief?'

She declared that she was not; and then she told me that she had made friends with the most charming young man whom she had introduced to her Amateur Dramatic Society at Blackheath. He had acted there in various plays, and she had taken him about with her to stay with several of her friends. After a time, it transpired that he was robbing them right and left, and, worst of all, he had made his largest scoop in the house of the parents of the young man she was going to marry. They naturally suspected her of being an accomplice of the burglar, and insisted on the engagement being broken off at the last moment.

Of course I saw that this cock-and-bull story could not possibly be true. It was obvious that this pretty young art student had quite another reason for wishing to get out of London, though I could not guess what it was. As she refused to give the names of anyone to whom we could refer for her character, it was impossible to enrol her in the Land Army; but I passed on her story, as she had told it to me, to a farmer near Westbury, who had asked for a couple of girls for seasonal weeding. He said that he would take the risk of employing her and her friend, as he had no jewels worth stealing; so he engaged them both, and they worked for him quite satisfactorily for some months before they disappeared once more into the unknown from whence they had come.

XVI

★ REVENANTS OF THE PLAIN ★

In a paper game, we were once asked to write down
what we thought to-day to be the 'Seven Wonders of
the World' and one of my selections was '*Stonehenge
with the twenty miles round it.*' I still cannot think of anything more wondrous. Perhaps the word 'miles' is too
feeble and inadequate, for Salisbury Plain is an In-
finity lying in an Eternity. The earth possesses vaster
distances; but none can be more utterly endless: and
on that Plain the monuments of the past are so ancient
that they seem to have become part of nature herself.
They belong as truly to the landscape as do the mole-
hills thrown up last night.

Speaking geographically, Salisbury Plain embraces
all the high land between the Oxfordshire Downs and
the Isles of Purbeck and of Portland on the Dorset
coast; but, in common parlance, it generally signifies
the twenty miles or so of undulating uplands which
lie between Salisbury and Devizes. Stonehenge stands
almost in the middle of this district; and when Pepys
wrote his diary in the seventeenth century, it appears
to have been divided from Salisbury by 'some great

hills even to fright us', though I know not where those hills can be to-day. Perhaps we are less easily frightened than the urban Pepys. This plain is now to a great extent a military training ground, and many a grumble is heard about the soldiers, and the way in which they are spoiling the countryside. Yet the plain is far greater than any army; and as one drives or rides over the seemingly level miles, passing, on the way, camps pitched on the turf, or regiments marching on the road, one looks back a minute later, to find that camp and regiment have vanished, leaving the Plain as serenely empty as before. For in those great spaces, the undulations are dwarfed into invisibility, although they are big enough to swallow an army on the march or a city of tents.

So Salisbury Plain remains the same great silent immensity, in spite of the many thousand men who train there every year. The plovers still turn and topple over it, their soft high-pitched voices blowing about in the sky; and the tiny larks still run swiftly up and down their invisible ladders of song. The wild flowers on the Plain are the smallest in the world, and yet, by their very multitude, they change the colour of the downs as one season succeeds another, and they fill the air with faint, indefinable fragrances.

These quiet spaces are profoundly haunted, and yet Salisbury Plain possesses few, if any, actual ghost stories. I know of no one who claims to have seen an apparition of what must have been one of the most beautiful and tragical funeral processions in the world's history, when for two nights and the best part of two days, Sir Lancelot and his seven companions went on foot the long forty miles from 'Almesbury unto Glastonbury', escorting the bier upon which lay, with face uncovered, the body of Guinevere the Queen. Sir Thomas Malory tells us that 'an hundred torches were ever burning about the corpse of the queen, and ever Sir Lancelot with his seven fellows went back about the horse bier, singing and reading many an holy orison, and frankincense upon the corpse incensed'. If strength and poignancy of feeling are the cause of hauntings, one might expect still to meet those figures on that long way of sorrow, but the beautiful vision has never been seen.

The Tattoo beaten by the Drummer Boy of Salisbury Plain is not heard to-day; and no one has seen the desperate chase when Mr. Dean, the farmer of Imber, pursued Benjamin Colclough, the highwayman who robbed him on his way home from Devizes market one October evening in 1839. Surely it might be expected that the turf would still echo the footfalls of those galloping horses, for the chase lasted full three hours, and only ended when Benjamin at last was ridden down by the farmer, and fell dead on Chitterne Down. There is still to be seen by the roadside the sinister grey tombstone-like monument which was 'erected as a warning to those who presumptuously think to escape the punishment God has threatened against Theives [sic] and Robbers'.

These intense personal emotions do not touch the great impersonal changelessness of the Plain. They vanish in it, as the passing traveller is swallowed up in those great spaces, leaving them still unalterably lonely.

H   [225]

No. The hauntings of the Plain are not personal, they are universal. The word 'Revenant' fits them better than 'Ghost'. Abstract presences seem to come and go upon the Plain, and they pass like the cloud shadows which move eternally over its still, impassible face.

Among such apparitions are those hounds of an uncouth and ancient breed which, within the memory of man, have been met pursuing their unattainable quarry in King John's hunting ground of Cranborne Chase. Thus they hunted, not on one day in any one year, but day after day and year after year throughout the centuries which we look back upon as a compact and definite epoch, and which we call the Middle Ages. Or again, there are the two white birds with widespread wings which never beat the air, who rise up from the spaces above the Plain, when a Bishop of Salisbury has died. They are mourning for no individual. They merely tell the passing of one more figure in that long line of Prelates who have sat in the Bishop's Throne beneath the spire which has watched the Plain for six hundred years.

And now comes my own experience, as impersonal as any; and so unlike the ordinary ghost story that it was years before I knew that it contained any element of the supernatural.

It was a dark October evening during the war, when I was superintending the Wiltshire Women's Land Army. In those unhappy years, my work was of all others the least unhappy, for it took me, not to scenes of pain in hospitals, nor to hear the endless whir of machinery in munition factories, but instead, to peaceful farms, where girls milked cows, or ploughed the fields, or harvested the crops. In those years I learnt my way about every part of Wiltshire, much of which had hitherto been unknown to me. That evening I asked the way from Devizes to Swindon and then drove on alone in my small two-seater car. It was between five and six, and a wet, dreary night.

After a few miles, I left the main road, and then I soon entered a very strange avenue. I was passing through a succession of huge grey megaliths, which stood on either hand, looming like vast immovable shadows within a curtain of softly falling rain. At once I knew where I must be. I was evidently approaching Avebury, that great prehistoric monument, older perhaps than Stonehenge and with a far more complicated plan. This part of Wiltshire was at that time quite unknown to me, but I had often seen pictures of Avebury in archæological books.

Like Stonehenge, Avebury was originally a circular megalithic temple, but unlike it, it was approached by stone avenues, extending in some instances for over a mile. In the old days, this must have added immensely to the impression created by the place; and now, coming upon it thus unexpectedly for the first time, I immediately felt its grandeur, and was dominated, even at some distance away, by the sense that I was nearing an ancient and a very wonderful place. By now it was raining hard, but I told myself that wet or fine, I must certainly get out of the car when I reached Avebury for nothing would induce me to miss this first opportunity of seeing it.

At the end of the avenue, I reached the great earthwork which surrounds the temple, and I climbed on to the bank. There beneath me I saw the huge stones, not standing more or less undisturbed in their lonely circle as they do at Stonehenge, but, far fewer in number than they once had been, standing or fallen in irregular formation, with cottages built among them interrupting the ancient plan. This did not surprise me, for I already knew that the village of Avebury was built actually within the old circle, its cottages standing rather incongruously among the megaliths, from fragments of which they were built.

This might be expected to spoil the effect of grandeur which Avebury should give; but on that particular night a village fair happened to be in progress. Although it was true that houses and people did take from Avebury that peculiar mystery which Stonehenge gains from its loneliness on the downs, yet I now saw that during the centuries, Avebury had gathered a new romantic character. The temple and the cottages possessed a unity, for the houses have not only grown up *among* the stones, they are *of* the stones. The vandalism which long ago hewed up the megaliths and made from them little houses for farm labourers to dwell in with their families, has succeeded in blending the one with the other. The old stones of Avebury are humanized as Stonehenge will never be.

And the fair that night brought out this aspect of the place. It looked right. The grand megaliths and the humble cottages alike were partly obscured by the failing light and the falling rain, but both were fitfully lit by flares and torches from booths and shows. Some rather primitive swing-boats flew in and out of this dim circle of light: cocoanuts rolled hairily from the sticks upon which they had been planted: bottles were shivered by gun-shots and tinkled as they fell to the ground. And all the time, the little casual crowd of villagers strayed with true Wiltshire indifference from one sight to another. Those great stones, the legacy of architects of an unknown race, had succeeded in adapting themselves completely to the village life of another day. I stood on the bank for a short time watching the scene; and then I decided that too much rain was falling down the back of my neck, so I got into the car and drove away.

I drove away for nine years, for that time passed before I visited Avebury again. This time I went there as a sightseer with a friend, and we walked round the embankment and looked at the village and finally went to get some tea at the inn. While we sat there, waiting for the kettle to boil, my friend took up a guide book which was lying on the table, and suddenly she exclaimed:

'Listen. What does this mean? You saw a ghost Fair when you were here before.'

Then she read to me that a fair had formerly been held every year at Avebury, but that it had been abolished in 1850.

So long had passed since the night I saw the fair, and so absolutely normal had it then appeared to me, that now I found great difficulty in answering the questions which at once occurred to my mind. How, for instance, had the people been dressed? As far as I could remember, very much as country people still did dress at the time I was seeing them. An impression remained of browns and other dark, rather dull colours—of clothes which toned with the rainy night. Then again, had I heard the noise of the fair or had I only seen it? I thought I remembered voices and music and rifle shots and the clicking of balls against cocoanuts, but how far away from me had those sounds seemed to be? I supposed that they must have sounded quite normally near, or I should have felt that I was seeing something uncanny. This I certainly had not felt at the time.

But now there seemed to be no doubt that in October 1916, I had watched a scene which must have taken place at least sixty-six years earlier.

The following year I was again at Avebury, this time as a member of a learned society which was studying the monument, for now I wanted to find out as much about it as possible. Sitting there on the bank, in a group of elderly savants, I told them my story of the fair. Their manners were too good to betray their incredulity, but one of them asked:

'By which way did you approach Avebury that night?'

'Not the way we came to-day. I came through the avenue of megaliths.'

'That had disappeared before the year 1800.'

So not only the fair but the whole of my experience that night from the time I left the village of Beckhampton a mile away, had taken me back to some time in the eighteenth century. I must have stepped back in time, as did Miss Moberly and her friend at Trianon, who in 1901 walked on paths, crossed bridges, and saw cascades, which had ceased to exist a hundred years earlier.

Mr. J. W. Dunne, the author of *An Experiment with Time*, in writing of this Trianon experience, says that, according to his theory of serialism, 'all our individual minds are merely aspects of a universal common-to-all mind, which mind has for its four-dimensional outlook *all* the individual outlooks'.

This is what I was trying to suggest in what I wrote above about the character of Salisbury Plain. Here, if anywhere, one feels as if one had been taken up into that 'universal common-to-all mind'. It is not a question of 'seeing ghosts' or of 'having visions': it is that sometimes, under the influence of that great spirit that seems ever brooding over the Plain, one's own little outlook is lost, and one is incorporated into something older and bigger and wiser than oneself. One knows what the past was like.

Of course I at once wanted to know whether or not that avenue ever did exist. Traditionally, as I have said, Avebury was originally approached by more than one avenue; but of the Beckhampton one by which I must have come that evening, there exists to-day no trace.

It was therefore with immense interest that I heard a year or two ago that the avenue was being excavated, that many of the megaliths had been found lying buried where they had fallen, and that these were being set up again in their original positions. I went to Avebury to see the work in progress.

Great was my disappointment to find that the avenue which had been replaced was not where I had seen it. Instead of going West from the temple, it ran South.

For a few minutes, I felt that I must wipe out my memory of that night in October 1916. Then I sat down to hear a lecture given by Mr. Keiller the excavator.

He explained that his reason for beginning work upon the particular avenue which he had now disclosed, was that one or two stones were still standing at its extreme end. These gave him his direction and enabled him with very little difficulty to trace its course. But, he went on to say, an even more interesting piece of work awaited him. Of all the old avenues, the Beck-hampton one possessed the most persistent tradition, although none of its stones remained. Here he would find no pointers to guide him, as the standing stones had done on the eastern side; but he said he was determined some day to find that avenue if he could. The audience who heard this lecture was so exclusively archæological that I had not the courage to rise up and offer to guide the excavators to the place where they should dig; but in spite of this cowardice, I hope that the day will come when I shall return to Avebury, there to see standing once more those stones, which, I believe, I am as yet the only living person to have seen above the earth.

XVII

★ THINGS PAST EXPLAINING ★

Some time after the visit to Trianon which Miss Moberly and Miss Jourdain described in *An Adventure*, Miss Moberly told me the story of the Bishop's Birds. There is an old and well-authenticated legend that when a Bishop of Salisbury dies, two white birds are seen, and this legend seems to have been very generally known in Salisbury in the 'seventies and 'eighties of the last century. By the time I heard it, however, it seemed to have passed out of memory. The older generation had ceased to think about it and the younger generation had never heard it.

Miss Moberly was herself the daughter of a Bishop of Salisbury and she said that an hour or two after her father died in 1885, she walked out alone into the palace garden. There she saw two very remarkable white birds which flew up from the ground and disappeared over the cathedral, going in a westerly direction. She described their appearance very carefully—the immense stretch of their wings and their dazzling whiteness; and she asked me not to forget this legend in case the birds should be seen on a future occasion and no note should be made of it. I immediately wrote down in my journal what Miss Moberly had told me, and then it passed out of my mind till the 16th of August 1911.

That day began miraculously. At three o'clock in the morning, my father called us to look out of the window and see Mars and Saturn in conjunction near the moon. The beauty of this sight was ineffable. The moonlight was melting into morning, and the moon herself had become a very pale, silver colour as she went down the sky. In the delicate between-light, the two planets glowed like warm gems of ruddy gold and we watched them as the light grew stronger and stronger, while they became fainter. It was a unique opening for a day which otherwise seemed to promise nothing outside the ordinary.

That afternoon I drove with the Wilton choirboys on their annual picnic and treat. We went to Wardour Castle, where I spent some very delicious and peaceful hours sitting on the grass beneath the ruins while the boys played cricket. The return journey was, however, a nightmare, and one quite outside the imagination of anybody to-day. We had gone in a horse brake, and the job-master was so careful of his beasts that he walked them nearly the whole way home. The first seven miles of that return journey took an hour and a half. The boys revelled in what they called 'a nice long ride', and they whiled away the time by asking riddles, which were mostly about pigs or policemen, and then by singing and shouting. I became very tired and I had been leaning back in my seat watching the sky for some time, when I became aware that I was staring at two enormous birds with very long wings. These wings were so brilliantly white that even their shadowed underside shone like water reflecting light. They flew up over the Hurdcott meadows towards the north-west, and they came up the sky with still wings which did not strike the air. It dawned upon me that I had never seen such birds before, and I called to the boys to look at them. As I did so, we drove under an avenue of trees, and only the smallest choirboy who was sitting next beside me said that he had seen them too. Our horses slowly walked their way to the other end of the avenue, but of course the birds were out of sight when we came out once more into the open. We talked of them a good deal on our way home.

When we got to Wilton, Albert Musselwhite, our Parish Clerk, opened the door of the brake for me to get out at the Rectory, and as he did so he said:

'I am sorry to tell you that the Bishop of Salisbury is dead.'

Curiously enough, I did not at once think of the birds. I had only heard the legend once and it was not in the forefront of my mind. Also, when Miss Moberly told it to me, I had taken for granted that the mysterious birds must of necessity be seen in the Close. I had there-fore no emotion but a startled sorrow, for the Bishop's death was completely unexpected. So much so, that most of his household staff had gone to London for a day's excursion, and his children had gone to a flower show.

My father had been very fond of the Bishop and he was much shocked by his death, so the dinner which now began was a most melancholy meal. My father

[235]

sat at the end of the table looking very depressed, and the various guests who were staying in the house knew not whether they ought to talk as if nothing had happened, or whether they must fall in with his mood. I tried to think of a subject of which we might talk without jarring too much on my father's humour, and as he was always immensely interested in natural history, I began on the subject of the unknown birds which I had seen. I had still completely forgotten Miss Moberly's story, but I described my birds very exactly and appealed to the company to tell me what they were. My cousin Tom Hunt, who was an admiral, laughed at me for describing albatrosses and declaring that I had seen them flying over the Wiltshire water-meadows. He said this was just another of my tall stories about my favourite county.

When I was going to bed, I suddenly recalled the legend of the Bishop's Birds and I hastily went to my diaries to find what Miss Moberly had said. I could not remember just when she had told me the story, but I found the passage after a long search, and then I saw that she had said her birds were 'like albatrosses'.

Bishop Wordsworth was a very great man, and it was fitting that the day of his death should be marked by signs in the skies: such things were more appropriate to him than words uttered by rather second-rate eulogists. I find that I wrote in my diary after hearing a succession of funeral sermons about this great man: 'I hate nothing more than undiscriminating eulogy of someone I love and admire.' One remark about the Bishop did, however, please me very much. Challis, the Pembrokes' gardener, said of him that he always spoke as if he were *thinking to himself*. This was very true. Bishop Wordsworth seemed entirely absorbed in his own deep thoughts, as if he was quite unaware of anything going on around him. This was not really the case.

One afternoon, the Bishop arrived at Wilton with a new setting of the 'Te Deum', arranged in a manner which he particularly liked from the liturgical point of view. He handed me the music, and asked me to sing it to him. It is a frightening thing to sing the 'Te Deum' through as a solo in the presence of a bishop, but Bishop Wordsworth's word was law, and I began in a very shaky voice, with Mildred accompanying me on the piano. The Bishop sat down at a writing-table and immediately became absorbed in the proofs of his edition of the 'Vulgate'. I sang about half of the 'Te Deum', and then I saw that his thoughts were entirely on his work and that he seemed to have quite forgotten me. I stopped. Without looking up, the Bishop said: 'Go on please.'

But I must return to other happenings that cannot be explained but can only be recorded.

I have only once visited the Land's End. It was Ash Wednesday and one of those blazing Cornish days which turn February into June. I drove out from Penzance alone just about noon in a small Austin car; and then I stood on the edge of that astounding cliff and looked out to sea. Stout Cortez could not have had a wider view. The Land's End is indeed aptly named. I stared across the Atlantic and as I did so I saw, some

miles out to sea, a town which was obviously a very
important place. It was a jumble of towers, domes,
spires and battlements. That must be on the Scilly
Isles, I thought, although I had never heard of any
great city there, imagining them to be nothing more
than a paradise of greenhouses. While I was still looking, a coastguardsman approached, and I asked him the
name of the town.

'There is no town there,' he said. 'Only the sea.'

'Surely you can see all those towers and spires?'

He looked as if he thought that I was quite imbecile,
and again he said that I was looking at nothing at all.

When he had gone, I made up my mind that I must
be looking at a mirage thrown on to the atmosphere
by that peculiarly powerful spring sunshine. Yet I had
a lurking hope that I had seen a vision of Lyonesse,
which some people say lies sunken under the sea off
the Cornish coast.

Later on, I learnt that I was not the only person to
have seen such a vision; and I myself saw it once more
a year or two later. It was a very different kind of day,
and the hour was late evening. I was driving with a
Miss Macpherson along the north coast of Cornwall, a
few miles east of Land's End. It was a wet and blowy
night, so the atmospheric conditions were completely
different to those when I had previously visited the
Land's End. Suddenly I saw again those towers and
spires standing immovable out at sea, while the rain
blew by them. I asked Miss Macpherson to stop her
car.

'Do you see anything over there?' I asked.

'Indeed I do,' she said, 'I see a city. I have often been told that from here it is possible to catch sight of the lost city of Lyonesse, but I have never seen it before.'

To hear her say the word Lyonesse pleased me very much, as this was what I had secretly hoped myself.

Some years afterwards I met Miss Macpherson and reminded her of this and I asked her if she had ever seen the city again.

'Only once,' she said: 'and then I was driving with my sister and she saw nothing.'

On the day of my visit to the Land's End, I had another rather incongruous adventure. When the coast-guard had gone away, I sat for some time on the cliff, until my eyes were so dazed with sunlight that I could no longer see the towers of Lyonesse. But what I did see was a very neatly dressed man, who clambered up the cliff from below and suddenly appeared within a few yards of me. He approached me very politely, and taking off his bowler hat, he said:

'Excuse me madam. Can you take photographs?'

I said that I could.

'Then would you oblige me by taking mine,' he said. 'I can never find anyone at these interesting spots who will take my photo. Be sure that you get the picture well in the middle of the plate.'

I took the camera and looked into the finder. The stranger had moved to the edge of the cliff and he had miraculously taken from his pocket a telescope, which he had extended and was holding to his eye as he looked across the ocean. Christopher Columbus himself could not have had a more adventurous air. I pressed the button and gave the camera back, but then I lost my head. I forgot to give the man my address and to ask him for a copy of that picture. I possess no memento of this curious scene.

Inexplicable things do happen to me, although I do not call myself 'psychic', as people say. One more peculiar anecdote shall now be told. I was lying awake one night in my room at the Daye House. The Park gates were locked so that no one could approach the house. It was midsummer, when it is never altogether dark. I heard something fall rather gently to the ground, and I thought it must be a book which had slipped off my bed. I leant out and looked on to the floor. In the dim light I thought that I saw a tennis racket. I knew I must be wrong, for not only did I not possess such a thing, but I knew that there never had been one in the house. I waited half an hour and looked again. It was still there. It *was* a tennis racket. I got out of bed and picked it up. Yes. In my hand I held a racket, and not a very modern one. It was an old-fashioned shape, slightly curved and many of the strings were broken. There is nothing to add to this story, for the appearance of that mysterious racket in my bedroom has never been explained. If it was an *apport* left as a joke by a passing spirit, I can only say that the sense of humour of those in another world is very different from ours.

BOOK III

★ WILTON ONCE MORE ★

PREAMBLE

★ THE DAYE HOUSE ★

*A*bout the year 780 *Alcuin was called from his Seminary in Yorkshire to become the chief master in Charlemagne's new schools in France. Then one of his Northumbrian pupils wrote a 'Lament', which can be read in Miss Waddell's 'Medieval Latin Lyrics'. Here are some lines from her translation:*

> *O little house, O dear and sweet my dwelling,*
> *O little house, for ever fare thee well!*
> *The trees stand round thee with their sighing branches,*
> *A little flowering wood for ever fair.*
>
> . . . .
>
> *Small streams about thee, all their banks in flower,*
> *And there the happy fisher spreads his nets.*
>
> . . . .
>
> *And there are lilies white and small red roses,*
> *And every bird sings in the early morning,*
> *Praising the God who made him in his singing.*

These lines perfectly describe my fourth and last home.

The Daye House had been the Wilton Park dairy, and we revived for it the old dialect name, when it became vacant and

[243]

*the Pembrokes offered it to us because they knew our love for
Wilton. Here I found again my lost soul.*

*Only the traveller who is well acquainted with the whole
width of the river valley lying between Salisbury and Wilton,
will choose to come from one to the other by way of Netherhampton; though there alone will he find unspoilt the broad
expanse of water-meadows. After Netherhampton he turns
into a little lane, shaded by silvery green abeles. Between this
and the meadow runs a very narrow canal, beyond which, far
away, the spire of Salisbury Cathedral rises on the skyline.
This lane follows the eastern wall of Wilton Park, and a gate
in the wall opens almost immediately on to The Daye House.*

*'The little flowery wood' is made of small winsome trees,
and from out of their tangle there rises a horseshoe of Scotch
firs. When the evening sun slants over the house, these great
trees leap into prominence—dark burning torches surmounted
by smudges of sombre blue-green foliage.*

*Here and there, through the trees on the north side of the
house, can be seen the glint of the water of the Nadder River,
flowing by a few yards away; and to the south the woodland
gives place to pasture fields dotted with trees and cows, where
rabbits hop in and out of their holes, and do their best to pop
through the fence protecting the garden and to eat up everything
inside.*

*The house is, as David Cecil said, both sensible and fanci-
ful. It might be a keeper's cottage if it were a little less elegant;
and if it were not quite so sober and workaday, it could easily
be one more of those small pavilions of pleasure which were
dotted about the park during the eighteenth century. Its somewhat fanciful name recalls the entirely sensible purpose for
which it was built in the 'fifties of the last century, and for*

which in my childhood it was still being used. The large octagonal dairy room has vanished. Gone are its marble floor and the painted Dutch tiles on its walls. Gone is that dramatic mosaic picture of a lion struggling with an enormous emerald green serpent which used to ornament the threshold. The dairy stood away from the house, with which it was connected by a straight narrow passage so that it looked like a frying-pan with its handle, and now the dining-room stands on the site of all that milk-panned playfulness.

On all sides, the grave little grey stone cottage breaks into surprises. Its high slated roof makes it look like a French farm-house, and one approaches the plain cottage door by a tiny colonnade, the pillars of which came from the pavilion which used to stand on the bridge near-by, and which was carried away to another part of the park to become the Park School. Windows from the old dairy are set into the rounded apse at the end of the dining-room, and the 'œil-de-bœuf' in the bedroom overhead is like a port-hole. The small turret in the centre of the house might be a pigeon cote. Its sides are decorated with little clusters of columns and with recesses which hold monograms. We added a long wooden room to the south-west corner of the house and now its walls are quite covered with roses and honeysuckle. G. M. Young once compared this room to the British Empire, saying that it began as a shanty and ended as a palace. When we first built it, it was undisguisedly a hut, its sections clearly indicated by thin lathes of dark wood, and in those days only the pointed roof protected us from winter cold or summer heat. Its walls were distempered in apricot colour and the mantelpiece was merely a rough beam of old oak found in a barn at Quidhampton.

Since then my friends have practically remade the room. Rex

Whistler classicized it with a ceiling and a formal panel above the fireplace; and he painted the amusing little wreaths on its beams as a surprise for me one night when I was dressing for dinner before a party. Geoffrey Taylor and John Stuart-Wortley laid the large squares of pale brown ash wood which now make the Floor; and the pictures are mostly presents from their painters. Willie Walton chose the piano, and bookcases encroach more and more on to the wall space. It is now a very pleasant room in which to sit, either alone or with a few friends.

XVIII

★ REMEMBERED VOICES ★

Visitors to the Daye House nearly always remark on
the green silence which seems to encircle it, and this
quietness is truly one of its chief characteristics. Yet,
outside and in, some of my happiest memories there
are memories of voices—the birds outside and conversation within.

Throughout the spring months, the Daye House lies
within a 'Charm of birds'. The park wall encloses a
bird sanctuary, and from four in the morning until
past sunset, there rises from the woods and copses in
the park a confused medley of harmonious jangling
songs. At this time in the year, the house seems to
become actually a part of the wood. It is possible to
distinguish the separate notes of those birds who
happen to be singing near-by; but beyond and behind
these, there continues away into the distance a widen-
ing circle of sound. The whole air is full of it.

Till I lived in the Daye House, I had no idea of how
elaborate is the language used by birds. Thrushes
especially have an immense vocabulary; and I copied
down one morning, as carefully as I could, the actual

words sung by a thrush in the laburnum outside my
window. This was his song:

Wit. Wit. Willy, Willy, Wit
Tchelitchef. Tchelitchef.
O-o-o-oy.
Dirt. Dirt. Dirt
Birdy, birdy, pretty birdy
Quick. Quick.
Give me a Liqueur. Give me a Liqueur.
Tch. Tch. Tch.
He's wheeling in tea and balloons.
See. See. See.
Be brave. Be brave.
Wor-r-rds. Wor-r-rds. Wor-r-rds.
Be a cheat. Be a cheat.
Give me some tea.
Just now. Just now.
I've been wet. I've been wet.
Not a word. Not a wor-r-rd.
Beer. Beer. Beer.
No he won't. No he won't.
Happy. Happy.
Wobble a woodle too.
Piano. Piano.
Cruel. Cruel.
Stand. Come here.
Did you see? Did you see?
Boys boiling in oil.
Willy cot. Willy say
Oh we know. Oh we know.
We go wheeling along.
Se-e-e. Where is he? See sir. See sir.
Let me kiss you.
Chicken beef and ham
Give him gurls. Give him gurls.

Is he going to scream! to scream?
What a spree! What a spree!

I cannot pretend that the talk inside the house often reaches this level of unexpectedness, but conversation has always been the chief amusement in the Daye House. This is because there is not room in it for a large party. When there are many people staying in a house, games will bring them together, but they only come between a handful of intimates. For them, talk is the thing.

During our first two years here, Mildred's talk made the charm and the character of the house; and now, nearly thirteen years after her death, it is hard to recapture and to express its peculiar quality. It was pitched in a very quiet key, yet never was conversation more full of surprises. So demure she looked as she sat there, and yet so unexpected were the things she said. People, their lives and their characters, were her absorbing interest, and she saw far more deeply into things than do most gossips. For gossip was what she enjoyed— talking about things which are happening to one's acquaintances; but with Mildred this gossip was threaded on to a tiny silken cord of inspired knowledge of the characters of the people about whom she gossiped. She cared for *them* more than for the things they did; and because of this their doings were to her more interesting and her talk about them was always illuminating. Mildred used to say that she never read a book, and indeed I seldom saw one in her hand. She was far too busy gardening or making things. Yet she seemed to *have read* everything and her talk was rich

[249]

with half-expressed allusions to her reading. Her conversation was infinitely more enjoyable to one whose
mind was quick enough to recognize these. It has been
said of her that she 'never finished a sentence, and if
she fell in with a courteous stranger who seemed to
expect to listen to the end, her embarrassment was complete. But those half sentences gave a nuance to her talk,
which a whole one would have blurred. She hated
explaining herself and never did. Her speech was like
music: its real meaning began where words leave off.'

Mildred looked at the world through very personal
lorgnettes, which she held a little bit askew, making
what she saw just odd enough to be funny without
interfering with the truth of her vision. In the memorial volume written by some of her friends after her
death, there is not one of the little studies which does
not attempt to describe her talk.

Dolly Ponsonby said: 'Her great quality was what is
ordinarily called a gift of sympathy, but which, in Mildred's case, I would call *interest*. There was nothing you
could do, or say, or write to Mildred—the smallest
thing—that did not interest her profoundly. There
seem, now that she is gone, so many things that one
could only tell to Mildred. To say that she was sympathetic is true, but does not exactly describe her attitude
of mind. She did not necessarily agree with you because she liked you and this gave her companionship a
savour. If she disagreed with her friends, they were
never offended, because she was so amusing, so genu-
inely interested and concerned . . . and with Mildred
we felt clever, amusing and attractive. . . . Certainly

[250]

she had the power of transmuting prosaic and everyday things into exciting and funny things. She could
extract amusement from a door-scraper. . . . She retained some of the absurd caprices of youth, enthusiasms
or dislikes for unaccountable things; there was the
charm of the unexpected and the unexplained.'

Gladys Meyrick speaks of Mildred's gift as a racon-
teuse, and Dorothy of her 'subtle sense of humour, too
much for everyday people who often did not under-
stand her'.

Yoi Maraini draws two pictures of Mildred talking.
'When I saw her last, a short time before she died, she
lay in bed explaining to me how the wireless worked in
her room. She described vividly the strange sounds she
heard, sometimes, late at night when, unable to sleep,
she listened. It seemed to me, in hearing her, as if she,
with a few words, brought the whole world—throb-
bing and palpitating with life—into her small room.
The trees outside, close to the windows, dripped with
rain, the light through them was sad beyond words;
with death so near we might have felt closed in, shut
away, afraid of the unknown. Instead of that, I look
back on that day as if, then, with her and through her,
I had seen and heard the cities and the forests of the
world in the laughing company of a gay comrade.'

And again: 'Sometimes when talking with Mildred
of merely passing interests, she would suddenly lean
forward, look into one's eyes and ask a question about
one's most intimate feelings. This was done in such a
way that it was not possible, for any sincere person, to
answer her evasively or with a lie. Under the light talk

she had detected something that was vitally important and she cared enough to want to discuss the matter. I can think of nothing that it would have been impossible to talk out with Mildred. The most tortuous paths of the mind, the most illogical, and the most inconsistent actions would have been understood by her.'

Christina Gibson 'would like to give a picture of Mildred half mirthful, half consumed with warm pity or sympathy, twinkling and teasing. . . . Her intuition was at times uncanny, like talking to a fairy creature.'

One of her nieces called her 'such an easy person to be alone with'; while another wrote: 'Another thing we relied on from her was criticism; she was impatient of dullness or stupidity and expected people to be what she was herself—gay, lively and amusing, and of "quick understanding". . . . She had almost perfect knowledge of what was going on in another's mind. . . . While she talked we listened and laughed or were deeply interested in her very definite but unusual ideas about people and all the many other things we discussed. Definite ideas, but she had a curiously indefinite way of expressing them; or perhaps only half expressing, and yet with it she was illuminating and made us think, and see things that we never saw before.'

Gwen Plunket Greene wrote: 'She could be scathing, mocking, and critical, full, too, of spice and wickedness. . . . She would listen with the *whole* of her attention, the whole of her mind absorbed. . . . Her constant occupation with the feelings and thoughts of others made her more understanding than almost anyone I have ever known.'

And Brian Howard tells how once he saw a very lovely view with Mildred. 'I admired what we saw and said so, but Mildred said nothing. She loved what she saw too much to do anything but smile. And the reason why I remember that spring afternoon, and I think always will, is because she smiled at me.'

Can these various extracts bring to the mind of those who will never know her anything of the savour of Mildred's companionship—rare in her speech, rarer still in her gift of eloquent listening?

Anne Douglas Sedgwick was another enchanting talker. Her conversation was greatly helped by her appearance which, with her white hair and bright-blue eyes, was as dazzling as a day of sun and hoar-frost. There was a New England puritanism in Anne's point of view, and though she enjoyed being with the younger generation, she wished them definitely to know that she was not *of* them. Her talk had the sharp glint of steel, with a sudden bright finality like the shutting of a knife. Anne talked beautifully about books, flying swiftly upon the essential in them, much as one of the birds she loved watching might fly upon a bright cluster of holly berries. She had a genius for seeing what the writer *meant* to say, even when he hadn't quite succeeded in saying it; and her knowledge of technique was such that it was truly illuminating to hear her pick out just the failure in craftsmanship which had prevented a complete achievement. She made one almost like a book the better for its flaws, and enjoy one which was not quite successful as much as one would have enjoyed a masterpiece. Anne was also a very delicate psychologist, and she could analyse the characters of her friends with truth, tenderness and a little spice of venom: in fact she brought to conversation just those qualities which she brought to her writing.

If there were no such bird as a stormy petrel, those two words would spring together to describe Elinor Wylie. Her appearance was beautiful, brittle and tragic, like 'The Venetian Glass Nephew' of whom she wrote, and she was extremely touchy. She was also the most egotistical person I ever knew; but egotism, if joined to intelligence, gives great point to conversation. Elinor's talk was always exciting, because one never knew when she would fly at a tangent into a sudden fury, or quarrel most violently with someone with whom she had, a moment before, been conversing serenely on some high literary topic. I remember one such instantaneous squall when she and Harold Acton were discussing Shelley's poetry. My attention wandered for a moment and then I heard them screaming at each other like fish-wives. She shrieked at him that Roman Catholics never read the Bible, and he hurled back at her that Shelley's face was covered with spots. I never learnt how these two poisoned darts came to fit each other as the appropriate *ripostes*, but they certainly both struck home and roused their opponent to fury. The mention of Edward Garnett's name was also quite certain to break up any conversation in which Elinor Wylie was engaged. He advised her not to write that fictional sequel to the drowning of Shelley in the Mediterranean Sea, which she

eventually published as *Mortal Image*. Mr. Garnett
thought that this might jar upon the feelings of some
of Shelley's admirers, but Elinor knew that she loved
Shelley herself so much that no one could be more sensitive about him than she. She could not forgive a criticism which seemed to her to put her outside the circle
of Shelley's true intimates, and to speak of Edward Garnett before her was certain to strike a flint which would
light a bonfire.

When she was not in this inflammable mood, Elinor
was a very poetic talker; her conversation was full of
uncommon words and individual turns of phrase. She
delighted to find poetry on side-tracks, and, picking up
some little casual allusion that someone had let fall,
she would play with it and beautify it till it became the
chief subject of the conversation. Then again she enjoyed nothing more than a serious discussion of her
own personal appearance. We talked for hours about
her each separate feature—her nose, eyes, mouth,
cheekbones, wrists, or hair. Each part of her became
like a separate person to be discussed and argued over
with heated agreement or disagreement.

Stephen Tennant is the most sparkling talker who
ever comes to my house, and perhaps the most amusing. He dances like a will-o'-the-wisp where other
people stick in the mud. Though his really kindred
spirits are the most exotic people he can find, he also
greatly enjoys a talk with some extremely commonplace
person, when he pretends that he thinks they mean
something which they never thought of in their lives.

He can be by turns poetic, malicious, and nonsensical. His talk is very pictorial and he handles words as if they were paint on a brush. When Stephen is alone with one friend he is often drawn to speak of very grave and profound subjects, and then he becomes unhappy, for he is never sure about what he loves and believes in, and he would like to love and believe in so much.

On the other hand, when David Cecil talks, his words rush out like rockets and turn into stars because of the fire of faith within. He is so passionately interested in his subject that he might be expected to become a monologuist, but as a matter of fact he is completely the opposite, and when he is in the room he makes everyone else talk well. He seems to care intensely, not only for the subject which is being discussed, but also for what every person in the room thinks about it, looking eagerly from one to the other, and drawing from everyone his best. David is the most sympathetic talker I know, and he always succeeds in making the conversation general. He also has a delightful gift for bringing the talk round, without any apparent effort, to any subject on which he happens to know that someone present will be able to shine. This makes the talk leap about the room with great variety and freshness. Such talk is for me quite impossible to report. Writing it down always rubs off its bloom; but even apart from that, one only remembers the outstanding things that are said in an evening's talk, although the little remarks thrown in by one and another have given it half its charm. They have in fact made it into 'talk'. One night, for instance, David made us speculate as to what really gave to a personality the quality of romance. This started a very good talk, of which I can remember only David's own contribution. He thought that a romantic figure is one which one thinks of, first of all, as walking alone and apart.

I enjoy nothing more completely than hearing David Cecil and Arthur Ponsonby talking together. It is like hearing an eighteenth-century Whig conversing with a product of post-war Oxford. Arthur's Whiggism is coloured with Socialism, as the Whiggism of Charles James Fox was affected by the French Revolution; while David Cecil's opinions are Conservative. But they don't talk politics here: they talk instead of life and of letters. It might be the historian of Melbourne talking with Melbourne himself. Arthur and David are of different generations, yet they both seem to belong to the age in which people had time, not only to toy with all kinds of knowledge, but to assimilate their knowledge before they began toying with it. These two men share a hundred interests, but each has his own manner of approaching them—Arthur with wit and wisdom, and David with lightness and learning.

Osbert Sitwell not only looks, but is a character from the circle of Horace Walpole. More than anyone to-day he succeeds in converting the lightest conversation into a polished formal art. He never dominates a conversation, but he controls it. Much of the best talk to-day is rather like colts gambolling freely in a field; but when

I

Osbert is there he harnesses the tricksome little creatures, takes the reins and drives the team. He decides
the lines which the talk is going to follow, though no
one seems to be aware that he has done so: then, although he leads the conversation, he brings everybody
else into it just at the right moment. So after an evening
with Osbert one can often remember the whole form
of the conversation, how it began, developed, and
ended. Osbert is also a master of the art of the *Conte*,
using the word in what must have been its original
sense—a tiny polished gem-like anecdote, made to be
spoken and not to be written down. He achieves this
perfectly himself, and he is also most appreciative of
other people's successes in this *genre*. He always remembers other people's good stories, and afterwards will
deftly seize the apt moment in another conversation to
call upon the teller to fit it in again.

Siegfried Sassoon is a wayward and capricious talker,
and if he finds himself among uncongenial people he
often won't talk at all, but sits apart in the spirit of his
own line:
'I have sat silent, angry at what they uttered.'
Siegfried is by turns violently intolerant, sympatheti-
cally appreciative, and savagely satirical. I suppose that
everyone talks best in an intimate circle of friends, but
this applies to Siegfried more than to anyone I know.
When he does wake up and begin to talk, his conversation is very racy and amusing. He makes fun of himself
as well as of other people and his descriptive powers are
quite astonishing. Siegfried is the best of friends.

One often reads of a richly stored mind, but one does not so often come across it. G. M. Young is an encyclopædia, but it is an encyclopædia which might have been compiled and written by de la Rochefoucauld. He not only seems to know all about everything, but that knowledge of his is all on the tip of his extremely witty tongue. He has a quiet presence and his mass of information never streams forth in monologue form. He takes no larger share in a conversation than anyone else; and yet at the end of the evening, one finds that it is he who has brought to it all its real substance and matter, its out-of-the-way bits of information and an intimate acquaintance, not only with the important events of history, but with many historical characters who have for centuries been forgotten by everyone else. Talk is always worth while when G. M. Young is there, and his least observation is barbed with wit.

Ottoline Morrell's personality is sybilline. When she talks, all that she says comes across with an added quality given by her beautiful figure, her noble features, her sombre eyes, and her deep emotional voice. She reads aloud very well, and some of the best talks with her which I remember have sprung up round about her reading of something or another. Ottoline has no superficial acquaintances. She is only interested in people whom she knows really well, and then she talks about them with wit and profundity, with sympathy and sometimes with bitterness. One evening at the Daye House, Ottoline read us a little study that she had written of Katherine Mansfield. She set her before us completely—body, soul and spirit. It seemed as if a little ghost-like figure had been created and was standing in the room; and at the moment when this impression was complete, all the lights suddenly went out. Her husband took a candle and held it to Ottoline's manuscript, and then she read on in the darkened room, the candlelight playing on her face till she too looked like a ghost, and her voice came from some remote distance. That is the kind of happy accident which Ottoline seems to call up wherever she is. She creates her own setting and speaks out of it.

XIX

★ SIGHTSEEING ★

I learnt the love of sightseeing from my father. By the time I knew him, it was the chief, if not the only, sport which he continued to practise. By then, he no longer walked up partridges, so instead he walked up churches; and, as ever, he preferred the chase to the battue. Indeed sightseeing itself he found less enjoyable than the process of reaching the sight to be seen; and the organization of our excursions meant an immense amount of preliminary staff work. The facile sightseer of to-day has no notion of how, in the past, we manœuvred and planned our approach to a ruin, a church, or a country house.

For instance, the distance from Wilton to Stonehenge and back is under eighteen miles. Nowadays, if a departing guest unexpectedly lets fall the remark that he has never seen the Stones, it is a simple matter to make a detour round them and to reach the station that way instead of by the usual direct three miles drive to Salisbury. But in my youth, we didn't throw in Stonehenge like that, as an unconsidered item in the course of a day's journey. We chose our date some time beforehand, because the horse must be allowed at least two days' rest before the tremendous undertaking. On the morning of our excursion, we packed two meals into the carriage and drove as far as Wishford, where we all got out, to 'save the horse', and walked up the long hill leading to the grass track which I believe was then the only approach to Stonehenge from the Wilton side. Then we got back into the carriage, and drove deliberately on and on. The steady fall of the horse's hoofs was silenced by the smooth short turf, and our passage would have been entirely soundless but for the squeaking of carriage springs which needed oil. The Stones came into sight at least half an hour before we actually reached them; and to-day it is hard to imagine the romance of that slow and quiet approach, travelling upon a green primeval road, to find Stonehenge at last, alone, unprotected by wire fences, and seemingly forgotten in the wide empty spaces of the Plain.

When we arrived, the horses were at once taken out of the shafts, and their noses were put into nose-bags. When they had finished their dinner they wandered about, on the ends of long hobble-ropes, making a dessert off the turf; while the driver smoked his pipe and went to sleep, and we listened, till we could listen no more, to our elders gravely discussing the origins of Stonehenge, and then we crept away and played rounders.

When my uncles and aunts stayed at Wilton in the summer, my father occasionally consented to interrupt his otherwise invariable rule of visiting in the parish every afternoon, in order to make an 'excursion' with us. It required no little planning. We used to start by train and get out at some station twenty or thirty miles away. Here my father's genius as conjuror first came into play. He never descended to the time-worn, and indeed futile, trick of producing a rabbit out of a hat; but he never failed to produce a wagonette upon a country road. And here, in the station yard at our first halting place, we always found the first wagonette. We clambered in, bristling with Alpenstocks and field glasses—Papa in his tall hat; uncles in soft felts; Mamma and aunts in cloth dresses and bustles; and I in the hard straw boater which girls of the period laid across the tops of their heads, much as the pancake man carries his tray. It was often pouring with rain, but we had not been able to change our plans because of the weather. Our arrangements had been made by post several days before: telephones did not then exist and most of our 'sights' were so far away from post-offices that telegraphing was out of the question.

We drove to our first destination, and here we generally dismissed our 'conveyance' and had luncheon at a wayside inn. We then inspected our first sight, while the beloved stuttering Uncle Bob Eden read aloud some appropriate passages from the *Wiltshire Archæological Magazine*, and Papa stood impatiently by, watch in hand, waiting to hustle us on to the next stage on our journey. This often meant striking out adventurously on foot across the virgin down; for South Wilts is a country of river valleys divided one from the other by green ridges, and it is often quicker to walk over the hills than to drive round by the roads. Pro-

2650

2496

8904

5704

tected by our mackintoshes and umbrellas, or else carrying them in bundles in our hands, we then set out to scramble up the slippery side of the down, holding up our cumbersome skirts, and turning now and again to scan the view through our field glasses. At the time of which I am writing, my elder sister was married, and as Mildred was always sick if she travelled either by train or by carriage, I was as a rule the only member of the party belonging to my own generation. Our route had been chosen to include various points of vantage from which specially good views of the surrounding country could be seen, so there were always several halts on the way, and our walk usually lasted well over an hour. When at last we began to descend towards the next main road, we saw waiting far beneath us the unfailing wagonette. It was not the one we had travelled by in the morning, and it came from a different village; for many of these excursions of ours took place on the lovely bit of country lying between the South and the Great Western Railways, so that our afternoon vehicle often came from a railway station on quite another line. Joyously we now crowded into our little wagonette to be carried to another inn where tea had already been ordered. After this we saw another church or two before catching a train home.

My father loved to plan and to carry out a complicated expedition like this; and one of the things which most endeared them to him was the fact that they had to be arranged so long beforehand. He hated sudden, scatter-brained decisions, and he nicknamed me 'Flibbertigibbet', because I often wanted to fly off at a tangent.

When we were at our Grasmere house in the summer, these expeditions were far more frequent than they were at Wilton because there we often had guests who had come on purpose to see the Lake Country. Blea Tarn was the first place to which our guests were taken. The uncle from whom my father inherited his Grasmere estate, had been a passionate Wordsworthian, and at some time in the 1870's he bought the whole of the Blea Valley, in order to save its solitude from being invaded by a projected enormous hotel. It is now many years since I last saw Blea, but I hope it is still:

> a little lowly vale,
> A lowly vale, and yet uplifted high
> Among the mountains: even as if the spot
> Had been from eldest time. . . .
> So placed, to be shut out from all the world!
> Urnlike it was in shape, deep as an Urn
>
> . . . .
>
> A quiet treeless nook, with two green fields,
> A liquid pool that glittered in the sun,
> And one bare dwelling; one abode, no more!
> . . . The little fields, made green
> By husbandry of many thrifty years,
> Paid cheerful tribute to the moorland house.

Not one line of that picture need have been altered to describe Blea Tarn as we knew it in the 'nineties. Uncle Alfred had completely preserved the farm and valley as Wordsworth knew them.

An excursion to Blea began with a walk over Huntingstile, to the village of Elterwater in the next valley. Lake Country walks must be taken Indian fashion, in single file; for the narrow footpaths are fringed by overhanging ferns and plants, and these are perpetually dripping from the never-ceasing rain. Stepping off the path is like stepping into a little mountain stream. So, one behind the other, we crossed the pass, and as we were slithering down among the stones into the valley, we saw, as surely in Westmorland as in Wiltshire, Papa's wagonette waiting for us on the road below. A slumbering driver sat on the box behind two slumbering horses, and the trio looked as if they had been waiting there 'from eldest time'. We then drove towards the Langdale Pikes, but after walking behind the carriage up the last steep hill, we always turned off the road to climb the pathless mountainside. In this way, we could descend upon Blea as Wordsworth did, on foot from out of the 'tumultuous waste of huge hill tops'.

The tenants of the farm were Mr. and Mrs. Weir. Uncle Alfred had been proud of finding them, for he thought that the farmer was indeed Wordsworth's *Solitary* in the flesh. The old man might almost have been a piece broken off from one of those rough stone walls which always meander across mountains. This was not surprising, as his farming largely consisted in mending the holes made in them by his sheep. His voice was the savage roar of some prehistoric sheepdog, and his language was more canine than human. He never spoke a complete sentence, but as he came up from the farm to meet us, he barked out a few unconnected syllables before he turned into the stable to hang up his coat. My father generally followed him there, as he enjoyed the conversation of this primitive man; though the rest of the family found that Mrs.

Weir's superior social gifts made her more accessible than her husband.

She was a cheerful little woman with a shiny wrinkled face and a very jolly smile, and she liked an opportunity for talking. Indeed she chattered away as if she was a practised conversationalist; and was far from giving the impression that she spent her life in a remote mountain valley, acquired by its owner with the sole purpose of securing it for ever as an inviolable fortress of solitude.

Blea Farm at this time belonged to my cousin, Harry Olivier, who was then a soldier in India; and Mrs. Weir's first remark was always 'How's the Maj?' as if he were some curious exotic magpie. She then gave us a most delicious tea, everything made by herself; but as she always called bread 'cake' and cake 'bread', it was difficult to know which she was offering and we generally found on our plates the one we least expected.

Wordsworth was of course our Grasmere hero, and my copy of his *Poems* is still filled with flowers which I picked in the garden of Dove Cottage in the firm belief that every tree and plant in it had been planted by him or by Dorothy. Papa often thrilled us with the story of his first visit to the Lakes, when he saw the poet himself at the gate of his house at Ambleside and found him not at all forthcoming. Then one day, when we were looking at Wordsworth's grave in Grasmere churchyard and saw written upon it the date '1850', Papa suddenly exclaimed: 'Why, he died years before I ever came here.' So ended a legend; and I wonder how many of the memories in this book are as imaginary

as my father's recollection of the poet Wordsworth.
One of my father's later sightseeing excursions came
to a dramatic end. He often drove to Pepperbox Hill,
a ridge about five miles south of Salisbury, upon which
stands Eyre's Folly, an eighteenth-century tower or
gazebo. From here the view is superb. Looking towards the south, there lies beneath the eye a wide
expanse of undulating New Forest country, smiling
and wooded, its rich luxuriant green flooded with a
warm and amber light. Southampton Water glitters in
the distance, the ships passing to and fro upon it like
little nebulæ in the Milky Way. And then, looking to
the north, there is a world of quite another colour. A
thin grey mist often hangs over it; but as the eye rests
upon this, there comes a sudden revelation—a point
where the haze freezes miraculously into something
sharp, clear and exquisitely soaring. It is the spire of
Salisbury Cathedral rising up from the broad shallow
valley where the five rivers meet. We often drove to the
Pepper Box, to walk for an hour or so along that ridge.
    We were returning from there one afternoon and had
reached the crossroads in the middle of Wilton, a few
yards from our own house, when a man driving a fast
horse in a high two-wheeled tax-cart shot out of the
side road, and tried to cross in front of us. His horse
was not quite fast enough, and there followed a terrific
crash. Horse, cart and man were hurled to the ground.
After a second's pause our horses set off at a headlong
pace up the Wilton street. The impact with the other
cart had smashed to splinters the pole of our carriage,
and this now swung between the horses, cutting their

flanks with every lurch and driving them to madness. The driver found that when the pole was broken, he had no control over his horses, and he conceived the magnificent last expedient of leaping off the box to go to their heads. He jumped: and was of course left behind in the road with several broken limbs. My brother Frank was in the carriage and he now climbed on to the box to take the reins, but found that they had fallen to the ground and were dragging among the horses' feet. There was nothing to be done. The horses put down their heads and stampeded. I shall always remember the frantic clatter of their feet, and the sight of them reflected in the windows of the houses we passed. They looked quite small.

This drive seemed eternal, though it really must only have lasted about a couple of minutes. A pair of horses running away between two rows of houses makes a noise which is surprisingly deafening; and in the middle of this hullabaloo, we sat in our landau, very stiff and dignified, no one saying a word. People flew to their windows as they heard us approach, and then they followed, running up the street behind us. The crash came at the next corner. The horses were killed: the carriage was broken to bits, and we were conveniently thrown on to the one patch of grass which was to be found beside our route. After the racket and rattle, there now came a sudden hush. We found ourselves lying in a heap on the ground, and as we looked at each other, we saw to our surprise that we were all alive. But both my parents had been badly hurt. My mother had broken her shoulder, but she did not lose consciousness for a minute. Papa had fallen on to his head and for a few moments he lay quite still and stunned; then he woke up to find himself in the arms of Whatley the builder—the first of the townspeople to reach the scene. I believe that a fit of fury is very commonly the first reaction to concussion of the brain, and this now seized my father, who angrily asked Whatley for a cup of tea—a drink he never tasted. It was an absurd anti-climax, and so indeed seemed the end of that most spectacular series of accidents. After that prolonged runaway and that terrific smash, there were no lives lost, only a few broken bones. But I think that this was the last of our deliberately planned expeditions.

The pleasure one derives from sightseeing varies very much with one's companion. It was my father who gave the tone to all those early expeditions among the Wiltshire downs; and since then I have found that all my memories of sightseeing are coloured with the personality of my travelling companions.

Zita James and I have made more than one motor tour in different parts of England, and she is an extremely scholarly and accomplished sightseer. Into the back of the car is packed her Travelling Library, which consists of a single bookshelf enclosed in a case. On these excursions, made with the definite purpose of visiting beautiful parts of the country, this case contains a row of Guide Books, mostly dating from the eighteenth century; and with these books as our companions, she and I have seen the country together in a very pleasant and unusual manner. The old *Itineraries* give the names of the owners of important houses on either side of the road; and so one immediately is thrown into the society of two hundred years ago. Other old Guide Books are the *Catalogues Raisonnées* of art treasures in certain great houses, which were compiled in large numbers in Horace Walpole's day. These contain many engravings and plans of the houses and grounds in their eighteenth-century condition. We sometimes found that our old Guide Books acted as passports into places we could not otherwise have visited. I remember one particular evening, we were mistakenly told that a very beautiful Yorkshire garden was on view for the Queen's Nurses' Fund. We left our car at the gate and walked more than a mile across the park, laden with huge tomes filled with drawings of a most elaborate series of water gardens. It seemed a very long walk, but the prospect of those formal cascades and fountains on terraces one above the other was enough to make us forget the weight of the books we were carrying. We arrived to find the gardens were not being shown after all, and we blundered into the presence of the owner of the house who was extremely surprised to see us and was at first inclined to join her dogs in shooing us away. But those heavy piles of books melted her heart, and when she looked over our shoulders at the enchanting pictures which had drawn us so far, she completely relented and allowed us to wander about the gardens until night fell.

Zita's sightseeing equipment does not only consist of Guide Books. She has a genius for picnics, and loads the car with bottles of out-of-the-way and delicious fruit drinks, and with knives and forks, plates and glasses. In the little towns and villages through which we pass, she goes into side streets and visits local dairy shops, from which she buys amusing food never heard of anywhere else. We eat this food and drink our fruit drinks in woods and fields, and are never dependent upon the roadside inn for a meal.

Anyone reading Sachie Sitwell's books about pictures and tapestry would, I think, imagine him to be a very deliberate and contemplative sightseer. The opposite is the case. He is magnetic. The moment he enters a picture gallery, he seems to be drawn swiftly across it by an invisible ray in the direction of one particular picture. Before his companions are even acclimatized to the atmosphere of the room, he has absorbed everything in that first picture and has shot across the room in another direction. Meanwhile the rest of the party are slowly assimilating the beauties of the various pictures one by one, and it seems that Sachie must have missed at least half of these. Not at all. In talking over the day, it appears that, far from having seen only those few things which seem to have attracted him, Sachie's eye has caught everything else which is worth while in the rooms through which he has passed. Sightseeing with him demands great quickness in the uptake.

Rex Whistler is the perfect travelling companion. He follows no prearranged plan: he is ready to respond to any unexpected invitation. When one drives out in the morning with a certain destination in mind, Rex soon wearies of the important road which leads to it and is attracted by some side road which appears to meander nowhere in particular. He turns into this. From it there diverges another byway far smaller than the first. Then yet another. Rex finds each one quite irresistible and we soon become lost in a tangle of little old roads, each narrower and more forgotten than the last; and more than once our roads have become footpaths which end in a single plank across a stream. Then we get out of our car and wander lazily through some very remote piece of country. Two or three hours later, we laboriously back the car out of the cul-de-sac in which we had left it, and regain our original road. So much of the day is spent in these unpremeditated détours, that night is sometimes falling by the time we reach our ultimate destination; and this adds immensely to the first view of a very beautiful scene. I shall never forget the colour on the walls of Milton Abbey when Rex and I first saw it after one of those long wandering days. A richly coloured lichen always grows on those stones; but that evening the sun was setting through a crimson mist and in this light the walls looked like some palace in *The Arabian Nights*, inlaid with gold and precious stones.

Another evening Rex and I arrived at a little chapel buried in a wood on the borders of Hampshire. We left the car in the road outside the rectory and asked for the keys. Armed with these, we penetrated into a deep dark forest, and felt our way along a very narrow footpath. It led to a deserted churchyard where, thrown wildly across the graves and shattering the tombstones, there lay an enormous uprooted yew tree, its roots and its torn branches tragic in the twilight. Behind it was a little fourteenth-century chapel. After fumbling for some time with the padlock, we made our way at last into a completely dark interior, upon the walls of which could faintly be guessed several seventeenth-century figures in high relief, some of them in clothes still brightly painted. We could not think what they were, and so we lit match after match beneath them; and as each little flame shone for a moment and then went out, we saw one after another the flickering faces of the long-forgotten members of the family of Evelyn the diarist. I have often been in that chapel since, but I have never seen so much there as I did that night.

On one of our many excursions up by-ways leading to footbridges, Rex and I once saw a very charming little rectory house. It stood high at one end of a tiny valley hidden in the downs, and curved lines of willows indicated the course of a shallow chalk stream. The Regency French windows of this parsonage house looked across the village churchyard into a distance which was indescribably peaceful. The memory of this place haunted us for years, and at last we learnt that it might be possible to buy our little fairy-story rectory. We decided to go to see it. It was a grey and dreary winter afternoon and of course we arrived several hours later than we had intended. I left Rex drawing in the churchyard and walked alone to the rectory. The garden was a wilderness. Sombre yews and laurels had encroached on to the white gravel path; and in the untidy grass patch in front of the house, could be seen the ghosts of flower-beds which must have been forgotten for many years. The front door looked as if it had never been opened. It had the appearance of a dead door left in some fragment of wall in a ruined house.

I gently pulled the bell, and felt sure that it did not ring. After a few minutes I pulled again, this time sharply. And now there sounded through the house the hollow bone-like rattle of broken wires, jostling each other ineffectively through the emptiness within. I heard immediately the approach of slow faltering footsteps, and a shaky voice said, '*Is anybody there?*' I announced my name in tones of bright friendly panic, and then began a prolonged fumbling and pushing of bolts and bars. It did indeed seem that the door had not been opened for years. At last after a great effort it gave, and opened with a dull puff of dust. A very old clergyman stood before me; and, unlike his door, he received me most hospitably, welcomed me with cordial smiles, and said that his house was indeed for sale as he was giving up the living. I fetched Rex, and together we made the macabre circuit of the dark narrow crumbling passages in this Brontesque and forgotten house, which seemed to be inhabited by two ghosts from a generation back. Lucy, the housekeeper, was deputed to show us round, but as we groped our way up and down unexpected steps at corners the old clergyman was always stumbling behind muttering such phrases as, 'I'm ill. . . . I'm going away. . . . They think nothing of this house. . . . They belittle it. . . . Lots of people want it.'

The house contained a great many small bedrooms, in each of which there was a dilapidated dusty bed, perhaps a chest of drawers, and sometimes a broken chair or two. The kitchen and larders were lordly—hung with pheasants, turkeys, rabbits and hares—presents from the churchwarden, so the old man said. But no one seemed to have thought of preparing all this game for the table: everything hung untouched in its fur or feathers. On tables and window-sills there stood dirty plates and broken saucers, and upon these were pieces of bread and cake, thickly covered with dust. A rancid smell rose from all this decaying food.

At last we reached the drawing-room, furnished with rather florid French furniture dating from the 1890's, the sofa and chairs looking as if they would break if anyone sat upon them. The walls were crowded with cabinets and shelves, upon which was a multitude of ornate Victorian china ornaments, all thickly coated with dirt. In the half-darkness of that gloomy afternoon, we seemed to have entered a house which had been abandoned thirty years before, by someone who could not endure the misery of living in it, and had suddenly left it, turning the lock behind him. Yet two people were still living there.

Only the dining-room seemed as if it might be inhabited by ordinary human beings, for here a fire was burning, a single place was laid and a bottle half-filled with whisky stood on the table. It was the only thing in the house which was not covered with dust.

We looked out of the windows: the view was infinitely appealing in its quiet beauty. We looked back into the room: it seemed that no one could ever again live within walls which had been so long haunted by that dingy horror.

When I drove through France a year or two ago with my nephew Tony, I was reminded of sightseeing with my father. For Tony too the enjoyable part of a journey is the actual travelling. He likes going from place to place, though he does not care much about places. Of course our actual means of transport could not be more unlike those of my father's day. The sleepy wagonettes had been replaced by the roaring Ford V8. That journey was the most appalling one I ever took, for Tony's favourite speed was eighty-seven miles an hour, and at this pace we rattled over pot-holes and ridges, and leapt the *cassis* which compose the surface of the celebrated French *Routes Nationales*, with their deceptive appearance of regularity. I was hurled about in all directions, and after a few days' travel, I was black and blue all over; but Tony sat solid and immovable, pinned in beneath the wheel. We called ourselves the Pea and the Cauliflower.

At this breakneck pace we rattled through the valley of the Loire, briskly looking in at the Renaissance castles, walking through miles of underground caves, the walls of which were stacked with millions of bottles of champagne, and spending an occasional day in one of those old local capital towns with their many-windowed palaces standing sheer upon the streets.

On that tour we went to Les Baux. Legend says that when Mary Magdalene and her companions had completed their miraculous voyage from Palestine, their boat drifted over the then flooded land of the Camargue and was stranded at the foot of a hill upon which Les Baux stands. We reached the place late in the evening and left our car in the village. Then we climbed up a little pilgrim's path which leads to the church. Here there is a tiny terrace, sheltered and still, from which one can look away over mile upon mile of quiet hill country. I turned from watching this great expanse and went towards the church behind me. The west door was open; and it was already dark inside. It was like looking into a cave, and I waited till my eyes should grow accustomed to the darkness. As I did so, a sudden light shone out in front of the altar, and above it there appeared what seemed to be a floating face. It had a quiet, still beauty. In form it was a rounded oval, and there was warm, red colour on the cheeks. The face was motionless, its dark eyes lowered and gazing on the light beneath them with an expression of tender care and watchfulness. My heart stood still, for my thoughts were fixed on St. Mary Magdalene. This must be her apparition. In a few seconds two hands gently raised the light and set it above the face. Then I knew that this woman was the Sacristan of the little church and that she had lowered the altar lamp, had re-lit it, and then had put it back into its place. She came down from the altar and knelt for a few minutes before the sanctuary before going to toll the bell. I realized that when I watched the Sacristan at her daily work, it had seemed to be the vision of a saint.

We were at Monaco on Good Friday, and there we saw the traditional religious procession which every year passes through the old town that night. It is completely medieval. No 'historically correct' fancy dresses recall a modern pageant. These people merely twist a bit of coloured stuff about their everyday clothes, and they become the people of Palestine.

A few hundred yards across the bay, the lights of Monte Carlo shone with the steady and unflickering brilliancy of electricity. So they had shone each night throughout the winter. That clear confident illumination missed the unique character of this one night. In Monte Carlo, it was just another night passing among a thousand; but here, in Monaco, it was Good Friday. Once again, as for hundreds of years past, there was no light in the street but that sent by flickering candles set on window-ledges; and through this semi-darkness the lights of the procession came and went. The streets are too narrow for spectators; and we moved from corner to corner to meet again and again these little ranks of grave and earnest country people, carrying their lights and their sacred emblems; or to watch the procession as it contracted itself sufficiently to pass slowly out of sight down some street which was even narrower than the rest. The processional lights were candles tied on to sticks and protected by large shades of cream-coloured cardboard. The effect was that of long-stalked round white flowers, softly lit from within. Sometimes the procession moved to the music of old Church tunes, sung rather waveringly by the thin shrill voices of choirboys—voices possessing so little carrying power that the sound went out with unexpected suddenness if the procession rounded a curve in the street. Sometimes there was an interval of heavier music, when the dull thud of crape-covered drums and the blatant harshness of brass instruments took their turn, playing a local traditional funeral dirge.

The circles of shaded candlelight, the children's faces

their eyes, and their singing mouths—all were round, sacred, and solemn like consecrated wafers. The Twelve Apostles were men in their ordinary working-clothes, and across their shoulders they had draped pieces of red, blue, or green cloth. The Holy Women had covered their heads with long black veils which fell to their feet. Above the Crucifix was a little tent-shaped roof of black velvet. The life-sized image of the dead Christ reposed upon a canopied bier. The golden statue of the Blessed Virgin was rigid, with no hangings either of triumph or of grief.

It took an hour for the procession to perambulate the many streets of the little town, but at last it reached the church, the façade of which was rather incongruously floodlit. Then the lurching candles, and the carefully borne images passed up the very steep and high flight of steps and through the west door. Darkness closed in upon the little twisted streets.

On the following day Monte Carlo took its turn and showed us a typical spectacle of the modern world. Its streets also wind round and about, and as in Monaco on the previous night, they were empty but for those who took part in the pageant. That day we saw an International Motor Race; and its music, like that of Monaco, was intermittent, coming and going among the curves of the streets. This time it was no sad and ancient music, but the terrific and shattering roar of the cars as they hurtled past our stand again and again. The course was fifty times round the town and it was a great feat of human endurance and skill. It was also a miracle that no one was killed. Our seats were near a bend, and once a car skidded there, blocking the road just out of sight of the other competitors coming up behind. Officials frantically waved flags. Spectators shrieked from the *Tribunes*, but five or six other cars had blindly hurled themselves upon the wrecked one before it was towed out of the way. It was very exciting, and very noisy, and our national pride was gratified by the fact that the three first cars were of British make. Nevertheless, I shall soon forget the Monte Carlo motor race, but I think I shall always remember Good Friday at Monaco.

XX

⋆ THE DEATHS OF KINGS ⋆

On the night of the 20th of January, 1936, my sister Mamie and I were alone at the Daye House, and we sat together in the long room through two hours which were till then unparalleled in history. King George was dying, and at ten o'clock a Committal Service was broadcast to all stations in the Empire. Science then achieved a hitherto unthought-of combination of community and seclusion. We felt as if we had been brought into the King's own room, which yet itself remained intimate, personal, and private. We also, in our room, were intimate, personal, and private, though we knew that our emotions in those hours were shared by other quiet listeners all over the world. Till a quarter past twelve we sat listening to the great tragic clanging of each quarter of an hour by Big Ben, followed each time by the announcer's voice always saying the same words: 'The King's life is moving peacefully towards its close.' At twelve-fifteen we learnt that the King was dead.

The universal emotion of the next few days has not been forgotten, and everyone repeated that never before had the death of a sovereign been received with so keen a sense of personal bereavement. It is true that King George's subjects had had opportunities of knowing their King which had not been possessed by previous generations. Everyone knew his appearance on the films and his voice on the wireless. He is said to have described himself as 'a very ordinary fellow', and this brought him near to the many ordinary fellows over whom he reigned. Those words of his may possibly describe the natural equipment with which King George set out, for he seemed to possess merely the ordinary gifts and tastes of a thousand of his subjects; but it was not that which won him the estimation he possessed when he died. The world had come to realize that there must be real greatness in a spirit which could thus take the elements of an ordinary man and out of them create a man who so stood out among his fellows. King George's subjects believed and knew that his only aims were the good of his people and the peace of the world. Other men have honestly sought the same things, but very rarely without some probably quite unconscious bias. Every man of experience in public affairs must have gained that experience somewhere—in politics, in a service, in a profession, or in a trade. Thus he naturally possesses a double loyalty: the King had only one —his loyalty to the public good.

The world marvelled that all this was realized so vividly by humble village people all over the Empire. They put it down entirely to the influence of the wireless; and if I had not re-read my diary of 1901, I too should have said that never before had we experienced

anything at all like it. But I found that what I then
wrote might almost have been a record of those days
in January thirty-five years later. In 1901 I wrote that
every cottage seemed plunged in personal sorrow, and
that Mrs. Gale, a woman of eighty years old living
in an almshouse, said to me: 'I think the Queen wer'
just overwhelmed wi' this war, and seeing Lord Roberts
last week brought it all home to her.' She had spoken
as if Queen Victoria belonged to her own family. And
then, when George V died, in 1936, an old-age pen-
sioner said to me: 'It's hard to lose a dear friend.'

I am horrified to discover how much older I am than
most writers. I seem to be completely out of date.
Almost everyone who wrote about the death of King
George was either a child or a baby in arms when he
succeeded; and none of them knew Queen Victoria
except by hearsay. They made up their minds that
when the Queen died, the world would doubtless have
felt her death to be the end of an epoch, but they were
convinced that her people as individuals had no sense
of personal loss. They said that this had to be, because
the Queen for many years had lived in such retirement
that nobody could possibly have thought of her as anything but a crowned and honoured mummy.

My diary in the last years of Queen Victoria's reign
gives a very different impression. We were all very
much aware of the Queen. A year or two before her
death I said to my father's old friend Sidney Meade
that I could not bear to think of outliving the Queen:
to which he replied, rather heartlessly as it seemed to
me: 'Then you'll have to die pretty quick.' I remember

being welcomed when I went to visit a racy old Wiltshire woman with the words: 'I couldn't be more pleased
if 'ee wer' Queen Vic herself.' It was the natural phrase
which leapt to her lips. And when the Queen died
three weeks after the beginning of the twentieth century, an old farmer said to me: 'The end of the century
seemed to mean nothing at all. The end of the Queen
is the end of everything.'

We first heard that the Queen was ill on January
19th, when the papers said that she was not well and
would stay indoors, but that afternoon Lord Pembroke
went to Osborne because she was much worse. After
that, we somehow got news many times during the
day, for I wrote in my diary on Sunday that 'the Queen's
illness was hanging over us like a dark fog' and that
she 'varied every hour'. All the 21st we were 'in a fer-
ment of anxiety about the Queen', and on the 22nd,
'we tried not to believe the bad bulletins that came'.
That evening, just after eight o'clock when we were
having dinner, we very surprisingly got 'a telephone
message' (from whom I cannot say) telling us that the
Queen had died at six-thirty. Telephones were then
evidently looked upon with great suspicion, for we
refused to believe the invisible speaker, till a telegram
came from Lord Pembroke with the same news, 'and
then the church bell began to toll at once'. I wrote that
night: 'It is impossible to believe. Impossible. Will
people in after days ever realize a quarter of what those
awful words mean to us? The Queen is dead.'

The next morning every man and woman in Wilton
from the highest to the lowest appeared in mourning—

such deep, overwhelming black too. In these days no one has ever seen such blackness.

Only a few of these black-robed people stood round the market cross to hear the Mayor proclaim King Edward VII, which he did in 'a melancholy voice, ending with *God Save the Queen*.' The crowd shouted 'King' but nobody knew whether they ought to cheer or not, till a doleful cornet struck up the National Anthem, and then everybody joined in.

Queen Victoria was buried on February 2nd, and on the previous day her coffin was brought from Osborne to London. We watched the beautiful sea pageant from Southsea Castle. The day was absolutely still and the Solent was veiled in a thin frosty mist such as Turner would have liked to paint. An avenue of huge black battleships indicated the funeral route, and in the still air the smoke from their minute guns hung overhead in billows of golden brown. It was late afternoon and the sun was already low in the sky, its pale rays throwing upon the sea a miraculous path of faint gold light upon which the procession was to pass. A dense crowd stood on the beach. Everyone in black. Everyone completely silent. They seemed not human. Down the golden way came eight destroyers all dead black; and following them, came alone the tiny Royal Yacht *Alberta*, with a motionless Admiral standing like a statue in the bows. An equally motionless Naval A.D.C. stood at each corner of the coffin, which could clearly be seen on deck covered with a white pall. The silent passage of the yacht, the immobility of the figures, and that great dumb, black crowd watching from the shore made the scene like something watched through a telescope from a very long way off. Other royal yachts followed, all of them larger and more important than the *Alberta* which had borne the Queen, and last of all came that magnificent white man-o'-war, the German Emperor's yacht *Hohenzollern*. When all was over, the dense throng which had covered the common and filled all the surrounding streets, moved away in dead silence.

Between the death of the Queen and her funeral, I see by my diary that I spent several mornings in working designs in purple velvet appliqué, which I sewed on to heavy black hangings for the church. I then covered the velvet with jewels. This seems to have been a very big piece of work, but I had so completely forgotten it that when these hangings were shown to me at the time of King George's funeral, I could not remember that I had ever seen them before. What I had not forgotten, but what takes up far less space in my diary than do those hangings, is that on the morning of the funeral the King's printers had not delivered our copies of the special service which was to be held simultaneously in churches all over the country. My father would never admit defeat, and he was resolved that no King's printers should prevent his expected congregation of eight hundred people from following the funeral service in Wilton Church. He therefore decreed that we should write out enough copies for them. I shall never forget that morning. Typewriters did not then exist except in the most modernized offices. No one possessed a duplicator. We had only our hands and our pens. There existed some horrible contraptions called 'jellies' on which it was possible to reproduce very uncertainly and unevenly about fifteen copies from one manuscript, and we also possessed what we called a printing press, which would make twenty or thirty copies in vivid purple ink. We collected a party of nine or ten of the young women of Wilton, and we spread ourselves over the drawing-room, the dining-room, the schoolroom, the hall and the staircase. There, from nine to one, we all wrote, rolled, pressed, squashed, and jellied; till it seemed that the burial service for Queen Victoria must be for ever written, rolled, pressed, squashed, and jellied on our hearts. But now I cannot remember one word of it. Thus was spent the morning of the Queen's funeral day, and by two o'clock, some four or five hundred copies had been written out. Almost every other person was able to have one, for more than a thousand people came to the service, crowding into the aisles when all the seats were full. The people were very silent except for the sounds of unconcealed sobbing.

I can find little in my journal about the death of King Edward VII, for, when he died, I was ill in London, so I had little opportunity of seeing how his death affected people. I remarked that Halley's Comet was then between the earth and the sun for the first time in fifty thousand years, and I quoted Shakespeare's words: 'The Heavens themselves blaze forth the death of princes.' A day or two later when I was well enough to get up and look at it out of the window, it seemed to be only 'a faint smudge of rather luminous cloud'.

The first time I went out after King Edward's death

I went for a drive in the park, and was struck by the truth that mourning is by no means a uniform. Women dressed in black differ more than they do at any other time. It is a commonplace to say that we all look our best in it, but, like most commonplaces, this is the impression of a one-eyed observer. What I saw then, and have often observed since, is that black clothes make women appear to be either duchesses or char-women. They are resolved to wear their rue with a difference; and this is fundamental, for while a man suffers the tortures of the damned if he is not dressed exactly like all his fellows, nothing annoys a woman more than to meet another wearing the same model as herself.

I was at Wilton at the time of King Edward's burial on May 20th, and then I noticed that the 'Church and churchyard were packed. People in every aisle. Everyone in black. Trains and trams all over the country stopped dead at the time of the burial.'

XXI

* WRITING BOOKS *

Ten or eleven years ago I woke up in the middle of the night with the idea of a story in my head. I had not thought of it before that moment, but it struck me as being a very good subject, and I immediately sat up and scribbled away for three or four hours. I thought at first that it would be finished in one chapter, but when I began to write I found that it was going to be a much bigger thing than that. Before morning I had finished two chapters of *The Love Child*—my first book.

Till that night I had never thought seriously of becoming a writer, and now I did not know whether what I was doing would ever be any good. I was sleeping badly at that time and I wrote practically the whole of that first book during those feverish wakeful hours when the body is weary but the mind seems let loose to work abnormally quickly. I have often thought that in wakeful nights one is quite another person to one's ordinary everyday self. One ceases to be human and becomes a tangle of the super-human and the sub-human. One is very creative and completely uncritical; an animal, but an animal of peculiar sensitiveness to spiritual suggestion.

The first draft of *The Love Child* was written in a few weeks, but when I tried to transcribe it, I found this a most troublesome business. The spiritualized animal which took possession of me in the night wrote a handwriting which was all but completely illegible; and each night's work took over a week to read. This erratic handwriting still flows from my hand whenever I try to write a book. The mind works so fast that the hands cannot follow it; and if the instrument lags behind, the whole thing is spoilt. I find that I cannot remember the end of any sentence that I begin. I therefore trained myself to compose on the typewriter. The typing of my first drafts is always abominable, but it is at least more legible than my writing of them. Though I am sure to have hit most of the wrong letters, the words come out at about the right length, so I can generally guess what they are.

Since the night when *The Love Child* was born, I have become a fairly steady writer, and people often ask me why I didn't begin before. I began to write about a year and a half after my sister Mildred died. We had been lifelong companions. She was an enchanting talker, and an inspiring listener. All the fun which one gets out of inventing a story and writing it down, all the pleasure which is given to the writer who finds sympathetic readers—all this criss-cross of give and take, Mildred and I had enjoyed together without the labour of writing anything down. We often told each other that we would write books, and she did indeed write one extremely funny one which she afterwards lost; but we found each other's companionship so completely satisfying that we sought no wider public.

After her death some dozen of her friends combined to write a little book about her, each one contributing an essay describing that facet of her character which he or she knew best. Harry Newbolt insisted upon my writing a preliminary essay in this book, which he said, wanted a more definite picture of Mildred's life than could be given by any of the separate writers, and that was really my first piece of writing. The *Mildred Book* was printed on a hand press at Shaftesbury and was illustrated by Rex Whistler and Stephen Tennant; and when it was finished, the idea of *The Love Child* suddenly came to me.

Alice Sedgwick was staying at the Daye House when I wrote my first two chapters, and I showed them to her in the morning. She liked them, and it was entirely because of her encouragement that I went on with the book. Afterwards her sister Anne introduced me to my first publisher, and so this gifted writer became, as she called herself, 'Godmother to one of your children'.

Long before this, while Mildred was still alive, we had once said that *As Far as Jane's Grandmother's* would be a good title for a book, and I had gone so far as to write down some suggestions for the first chapter. This phrase had always been one of our family sayings. My elder brothers used to walk with Jane, their nursery-maid, to visit her grandmother, who lived in a cottage in the Hare Warren, a mile and a half away. It was the longest walk they ever took in those days and it became our family measure of distance. I now saw it as a spiritual measure, and used it to suggest the story of a girl whose grandmother was so dominating a personality that all her life she could never walk beyond the sphere of that overpowering influence.

I liked this subject. The autocratic grandmother was a type I knew well in my father and his sisters. It is a character which charms me, mostly because I could never be at all like it myself. Such characters are rare to-day. They suggest a life lived in a secure and unshakable setting. The tides of varying opinions may sweep to and fro outside it, but all the time it remains completely watertight. The house of such people is indeed built upon a rock. Fashions and opinions may change, the world look this way and that, uncertain what to believe or how to act, but within those impenetrable walls, life goes on as before. The master of the house remains its master. A personality such as this sounds harsh and forbidding, and it may be so at heart, but in the case of my father, I had seen it veiled in an outer garment of courteous old-fashioned manners, which simply made him impossible to argue with. If one ever attempted such a thing, he could always finally and definitely place one in the wrong. The longer one knew him, the more one came to see that his system *worked*. He had made his own conception of life as he had decided that it should be lived, and he continued to live in that way, whatever the world around him said, thought, or did. The first reaction of youth was naturally to rebel against this overmastering authority; but in order to rebel successfully, the rebel must have his own conception of life, equally complete and equally believed in. Not many people possess this.

[293]

The story of Jane with her few ineffectual struggles is really a symbolic picture of life in my own father's house.

I notice that many of my friends feel obliged, when publishing a book, to lay their hand on their heart, and solemnly to protest that it contains no portraits—that all the people described in it are dead or have never lived. I have never done this because I don't think that real life fits into fiction. When a living person or an actual event is inserted into a novel, it seems completely out of scale and quite unreal. It is a common thing to hear people say to a writer that there is one person, or one episode in his book which really is beyond belief; and the answer nearly always is that that is the only thing in the book which is taken from real life. For my own part I have never been able to get a slice of actual life into a novel: it simply won't go in. Real life comes into fiction at its two extremes. It first gives the fundamental idea from which a book will grow; and then, from it one can often select those little gestures and unconscious movements by which people express emotion and which often give them their individuality.

When we lived in the Close at Salisbury, I was never tired of observing how much the beauty and character of the houses there affected the people who lived in them. This was the fundamental idea of *The Seraphim Room*. It came from Salisbury Close, though not one of the people in that book had ever lived there.

Then again, I have known a good many dwarfs in my life, and I have always noticed that there are certain mental and moral characteristics which seem to spring

[294]

from dwarfishness. Then I have further observed that these characteristics are sometimes stronger in those members of a family who are not themselves dwarfs than they are in the dwarfs themselves. *Seeing* a dwarf appears to affect one more than *being* a dwarf. This is the idea at the root of *Dwarf's Blood*, but again, none of its characters are portraits.

My father owned a collection of family papers which had at one time been carried off by a footman. Among them this man had discovered an ancient patent of nobility given to a member of the Olivier family. The adventurous footman adopted the title and travelled all over Europe as a marquis. This amusing idea was at the bottom of *The Triumphant Footman*.

Fiction is for me far easier to write than history or biography, for in fiction one generally escapes all the labour of research. It was almost by chance that I wrote two biographies. The first was the *Life of Alexander Cruden*, a name known to most people, though hardly anyone knows more about him than his name. People murmer: 'Cruden's *concordance*,' though the phrase often conveys nothing at all to their minds.

I had always wanted to know more about Cruden. When I was a little girl, I was one day sitting on the floor in my father's study, when my mother came into the room and took from the shelf an enormous tome. She studied it for a few moments and as she pushed it back into the shelf, she said, with a dramatic gesture:

'Right as usual. That man never made a mistake. No wonder he went mad.'

I was profoundly impressed, and I knew the book

was Cruden's *Concordance*. Later on, I often remembered
those words and wondered whether Cruden really had
been mad, and if so, whether the *Concordance* had driven
him out of his mind. At last I found his name by chance
in the *Dictionary of National Biography*. There I learnt
that Cruden did indeed go mad, not only once, but
three times, and that each time it was a love affair which
drove him demented. In the British Museum I read the
long and elaborate journals which Cruden kept in the
Mad House. I read of his instalment as Reader in
French to the Earl of Derby at Halnaker Castle, and
of how he had lost his situation because he could not
pronounce a single French word. I read of his dramatic
love affairs and of the superhuman effort by which he
saved a poor sailor boy from the gallows on the very
morning fixed for his execution. I found an account of
the interview between the absurd yet inspired little
bookseller and that most charming of eighteenth-century queens, Caroline of Anspach. There was certainly
much more in the life of Alexander Cruden than the
compilation of a *Complete Concordance to the Scriptures*.
His was a most entertaining life to write.

And when Peter Davies asked me to contribute a
volume to his series of short biographies I felt obliged
to write the life of Mary Magdalen, which was not
really a biography at all, but a work built up from a
number of the beautiful imaginative and poetic lives of
the Saint written during the Middle Ages.

The book has no value as history. What historical
character it may possess lies in the picture it gives of
the devotional mind in the Middle Ages. There I can

declare that it is faithful and true; for every episode is taken from one or other of the old lives of the Saint which I had long loved to read. Mary Magdalen was fortunate in that her earliest biographers appeared in Provence, where her legend had persisted since the first or second centuries. Then, when these traditional stories began to be written down, the first springs of romance were already rising in the land of the Troubadours. Devotion and Beauty mingled with a simplicity and ease which has seldom been approached. In my *Life of Mary Magdalen*, I aimed at introducing this sacred Fairyland to those of my contemporaries who did not yet know it.

Most autobiographies make one wonder at the number of distinguished people known to their writers. Indeed they often seem to have no other acquaintances. Yet I have often thought that many of the humble and unknown people I knew in my childhood and youth are equally worth describing. More so perhaps; for some of these simple Wiltshire men and women were of a type which is fast disappearing. Their lives, their tastes, and their interests were limited in area as those of few people to-day are limited. The Wilton I first remember was a Provincial town in a sense that no town can be in this twentieth century; when the stream of modern life pours through it in motor cars, and the polished accents of wireless announcers sully the purity of its ancient tongue. When they beat the bounds of the borough in those old days they were beating something with a spiritual, as well as a tangible existence. It is something of this old local life that I have tried to recall in *Without Knowing Mr. Walkley*; and if I fail to interest my readers in the old Wilton characters I have described, the fault is in my pen, not in my subject.

XXII

⋆ MIGRANTS ⋆

I often think that the politest man I ever knew was Frank Brown, who was the bailiff at the Home Farm when we were children. He was a slim, dapper little man, in appearance more like a solicitor than a farmer; and though he looked about fifty, I believe he was never under eighty. On Sunday mornings he always appeared in Netherhampton Church supremely dressed in a black cut-away coat, pale-grey trousers with pin stripes, a tall hat, and gloves of thick lavender suède. His politeness was chiefly shown in those gloves. During the service he took them off and laid them very neatly on the shelf in front of him; and before leaving the church he put them on again and very slowly buttoned them up, for he always walked some way into the park with my father after the service, and according to Frank Brown's code, gloved hands were essential when walking with rectors. Then came the crux. Some of the family often walked through the park to meet my father, and we sometimes came upon the two men quite suddenly round a corner, or we sat waiting under a tree in the shade, so that they did not see us till they were actually upon us. Then Frank Brown feverishly began to unbutton his right hand glove in order to shake hands with the ladies. It often stuck, and it always took a long time; but while the frantic struggle went on, Mr. Brown never looked at us. He remained bowed over his own hand, and we, too, looked at the distant view, appearing not to see his agonized exertions. When at last the glove was off, each party started up appearing to perceive the other for the first time, and then we cordially shook hands.

Frank Brown was an enthusiastic naturalist and sportsman, which greatly endeared him to my father; and when they took these Sunday walks together, they were constantly reminding each other of historic runs with the different Wiltshire packs, or they told stories of bustards, badgers, and otters.

Frank Brown had a very good story about a fox, which he once saw trotting along, within its mouth a curious white thing. At first Mr. Brown could not make out what this was, but after a time he saw that it was rather a large piece of sheep's wool. He watched the fox till he reached one of the dew ponds on the down, and there he turned round and went backwards into the water, walking cautiously towards the deepest part till he was entirely submerged except for his nose and mouth, which projected from the water, still holding the piece of wool. Then he stood still. Frank Brown was so much interested that he crept near to the water's edge and looked on, while the fox was far too busy to notice him.

After a few minutes some black specks appeared on

the wool. These increased in number till they completely covered the white surface. Something was coming up out of the water. Then Mr. Brown saw that this was an army of fleas, and that the fox had devised this cunning way of driving his enemies off his body. He waited patiently till the black mass had ceased to increase in size, then he dropped the piece of wool into the pond, walked out of the water and trotted away.

Wiltshire is like that fox, and so are Wiltshire people. Ever since the dawn of history, successive migrants have crossed it, been shaken off, and have been forgotten. Yet they continue to come. The natives endure them for a time, seeming to ignore them and to go on mouching about the streets, leaning against the walls, hanging over the gates and staring vacantly over bridges into the water. Then they wake up, and shaking off the alien visitors, they go on as before, forgetting all about them.

To the migrant flitting by on his gaily coloured wings, the corduroy-clad native will always appear drab and dreary. The Cockney thinks the Wiltshireman unendurably slow and stupid. He is not such a fool as he looks, as was proved once for all by the story of the Moonrakers, which gave the Wiltshireman his nickname. Although this story is very familiar, I will tell it again.

The village of Bishop's Cannings lies almost exactly in the middle of the county, and many of the best Wiltshire stories are told of the Bishop's Cannings men. One evening in the early nineteenth century, an exciseman from London was driving over the downs in the direction of Devizes, and as he neared the village of Bishop's Cannings, he saw a group of men in charge of a float which was drawn by a donkey. They had pulled up beside a dew-pond and were busily raking the water with their long wooden hay rakes. The exciseman stopped, and in his refined London accent he asked these yokels what in the world they were doing. The stupid fellows pointed to the reflection of the full moon in the pond—large, yellow, and round.

'Zomebody bin and lost a cheese,' they said, 'and us be a-raking of un out o' thic thur pond.'

This was an excellent story for the exciseman to produce an hour later in the parlour of 'The Bear' at Devizes, and never had he told one with more success. The roars of laughter which received it came from an audience in which every man was well aware that the Bishop's Cannings pond was a recognized dumping-place for the casks of whisky which were regularly smuggled from the Dorset coast along the green down roads. The 'moonrakers' were well known to all the company present, and this was the kind of joke likely to be appreciated by the 'slow' people of Wiltshire.

Earlier migrants came seeking to impress themselves on the faces of the county. The Romans threw five unflinching roads across the country from the ramparts of Old Sarum, while others took their undeviating course from end to end of the county, going from Winchester to Marlborough or the Mendip Hills, or from Silchester to Blandford in Dorset. Most of these roads have been reabsorbed into what now looks like the virgin soil of down or meadow, though here and there the stone paving is still lying concealed only a few inches underground. I have seen it brought to light a few paces to the north of the present Bath Road, just where it passes the Avebury Sanctuary; and once when I was driving near Wishford with G. M. Young, he sensed that we were near the spot where the Roman Road would have crossed the lane on its way from Old Sarum to Grovely. A short search revealed in the level meadow-land a straight course, only a few feet wide, where we seemed to recognize the impress of another levelling two thousand years old. Mr. Young took the great iron key of the hatches and struck it two or three times into the earth, and then his tool rang on a hidden pavement of stone. Across the sodden marsh of the then undrained Wylye valley, the Romans had driven their hard unshakable road; and it was still there.

The road builders must once have been there in their thousands, disturbing the quiet of the country with the noise of their hammers and the sound of voices talking a foreign language. The beauty of Wiltshire must then have seemed defaced for ever by the tents and the hutments, and by the great heaps of road-building materials which were carried along in creaking carts, to be thrown out by the roadside. It must have seemed that Sarum and Shaftesbury were becoming suburbs of Rome. But no. All those men have gone and the green grass has surged again over the stones which they laid down with so much turmoil and dust.

Some centuries later, the Normans ruled over Wiltshire, building their proud castles upon the ancient earthworks, which had been planted on all the key

places of the county by long dead military geniuses—
members of tribes whose very names had been forgotten. The county belonged to the men who owned
those strongholds, or so it must then have appeared.
The fortress of Old Sarum would have looked terribly
strong to the men who stared up at it from their farm-
steads in the Avon valley; and the arrogant soldiers
who garrisoned it thought they could be as rude as
they liked to the bishops and clergy who dared to take
the part of their Saxon flocks. But one day those soldiers were a bit too rude. It must have been an excellent joke in the Mess, when, one spring evening, the
Rogation procession was so long making its circuit
that the Bishop and his canons failed to reach the gates
at the top of the long hill, before the Curfew bell had
sounded. The soldiers pulled up the drawbridge and
the Churchmen were shut out for the night. But they
had their pride too. They abandoned the old city to
the garrison, and in a meadow in the valley below they
built the elegant slim cathedral which soon superseded
the old castle as the principal landmark in the county.
The townsmen followed the Clergy. The new city of
Sarum rose outside the Close, and the migrants were
left isolated in their eyrie. Gradually the castle and the
city and the old cathedral fell into ruins, and were for
centuries the favourite stone quarry of village builders
for miles round.

Wiltshire was again the fashion in the Plantagenet
days, when the kings kept their Court at Clarendon.
This legendary palace had a unique distinction in those
warlike times, for it was completely unfortified, and

was a palace of pleasure alone. The soldiers remained at Old Sarum some six miles away, and here, on the slope of the hill above the Avon valley, there arose this wide-spreading lofty building, its walls supported without by colossal buttresses and painted within by some of the leading mural painters of the day, who founded here a far-famed school. The floors of the palace were paved with fantastic tiles, worked in elaborate patterns; and from its gates, companies of kings rode forth to hunt in the forest, or to joust on the tournament ground above Bemerton. Edward III hunted here with three kings after the battle of Poitiers —John of France, Philip of Navarre, and David of Scotland. Ridiculous courtiers brought into the country the latest fashions from town. The men had long points to their boots and the women long points to their hats, and in the palace they played their games, sang their songs, and composed their verses, completely ignoring the other life which was going on around them. In the farms the Wiltshire people were wearing clothes which were cut in almost the same pattern as those their predecessors had worn two hundred years before, and they were carrying out the same tasks in exactly the same manner. Then that romantic palace vanished, and vanished more mysteriously than any other great building in the world. To this day no one knows what happened to it. It just ceased to be, leaving behind it the tradition of a gold chair buried in its vaults, and of the path by which St. Thomas à Becket walked daily from his cure at Winterbourne in the valley to say Mass in the Palace

Chapel—a path which since then has always remained miraculously green. Once again Wiltshire, with its unchanging steadfastness, surged over the outstanding buildings thrown up on the high ground by those passers-by. The stones of the palace were absorbed into the humble houses of the surrounding villages, and for many years its foundations were hidden beneath a tangle of green growth. Only in the past few years has the plan of Clarendon Palace been rediscovered by Tancred Borenius and his wife, whose zeal and knowledge have rescued it from the oblivion to which Wiltshire persists in consigning her migrants.

During the past thirty years, armies of soldiers have crossed Salisbury Plain. During the war, there were several parts of Wiltshire in which one drove for nine and ten miles at a stretch through continuous camps. The ugly ramshackle buildings of wood and tin completely swamped for the time those villages which had always been so remote with their little thatched houses and their large quiet churches. One then felt that Wiltshire must be ruined for ever. But now all those huts have gone. The grass has grown over the scorched untidy ground which they left behind them. Here and there can be seen a fading memento of the war-time settlements of the Colonial battalions which thronged the Wiltshire villages while the war lasted. It may be the faded and washed-out remnant of what was once a big and gaudy advertisement painted on the side of a house, to announce that a cinema would be open three times in the day; or there are regimental badges cut through the turf into the chalk on the downs, in the manner of the Wiltshire white horses. These were a constant interest to the men who cut them, but they are now very erratically 'scoured'. And then one comes across here and there a war-time cemetery, or the graves of strangers in a village churchyard.

There are, of course, still many soldiers on the Plain, and their camps look solid and permanent, but so must have looked the great Norman castles which have gone. To the people of Wiltshire, the soldiers will always be passers-by.

Wiltshire is now fashionable again, and a great many amusing parties are given here by people who delight to say that the county is now as gay as London, and gay in the same way. They would like it to become a suburb of London, although it long ago refused to become a suburb of Rome. Like the earlier migrants, these migrants of to-day would find the real Wiltshire life extremely boring, and as a matter of fact they never touch it. They could not do so, unless they were content to settle down in a Wiltshire village, to live there year in and year out and to have a great many children in it. None of them wish to do this, and until they do so, the natives will still adopt towards them the traditional Wiltshire attitude of: ' 'Ere's a stranger. 'Eave 'alf a brick at un.'

A friendly young new-comer to a village in the county made a practice of going to the inn in the evenings to talk with the men sitting in the bar. There lived in the village a rascally old horse-coper, who was very racy of the soil. And one of his friends invited him to come in one evening to meet the new-comer.

He shook his head.

'T'ooden do no good to I to be seen wi' that lot,' was all he said.

It is still a case of the fox and the fleas.